To the memory of Suzanna and Artie Cheekie
and all the Sayisi Dene
who died in Churchill between 1956 and 1973.

When I was a little girl, every night at bedtime, my mom made us say the Lord's Prayer in Dene. She would tuck us in and tell us we had to be quiet or *e'thzil* would hear us. The word *e'thzil* means "night spirits." Night spirits are the spirits of dead people. — Ila Bussidor

I dream of an eagle
Forever coming to me with messages of strength
Always in friendship and kindness.
I touch the great sacred bird of spirit.
He cares for me, each time I vision him.
He lets me carry him.
He gives me his sacred feathers.
He walks with me.
I am not afraid of him.
I believe he is my guardian.
The spirits of my father and mother
Beside me in my times of pain.

— Ila Bussidor

CRITICAL STUDIES IN NATIVE HISTORY
ISSN 1925-5888

NIGHT SPIRITS

THE STORY OF THE RELOCATION OF THE SAYISI DENE

ILA BUSSIDOR AND ÜSTÜN BILGEN-REINART

THE UNIVERSITY OF MANITOBA PRESS

Night Spirits: The Story of the Relocation of the Sayisi Dene
© Ila Bussidor and Üstün Bilgen-Reinart 1997

23   22   21   20   19   4   5   6   7   8

University of Manitoba Press
Winnipeg, Manitoba, Canada
Treaty 1 Territory
uofmpress.ca

Cataloguing data available from Library and Archives Canada
Critical Studies in Native History, ISSN 1925-5888; 10
ISBN 978-0-88755-643-2 (PAPER)
ISBN 978-0-88755-348-6 (PDF)

Cover and internal design: Steven Rosenberg/Doowah Design
Maps: Weldon Hiebert
All photos taken at Camp-10 and Dene Village are courtesy of Skip
Koolage. All photos taken at Tadoule Lake and North River courtesy of Ila
Bussidor. Front cover photo: Anglican Diocese of Keewatin; back cover
photo: HBCA.

The publishers would like to thank Professor William (Skip) Koolage for
permission to reprint his photographs of Camp-10 and Dene Village, and
Virginia Petch for permission to reproduce a version of her map of the
traditional lands of the Sayisi Dene.

Printed in Canada

The University of Manitoba Press acknowledges the financial support for
its publication program provided by the Government of Canada through
the Canada Book Fund, the Canada Council for the Arts, the Manitoba
Department of Sport, Culture, and Heritage, the Manitoba Arts Council,
and the Manitoba Book Publishing Tax Credit.

Funded by the Government of Canada   Canadä

CONTENTS

ACKNOWLEDGEMENTS

We gratefully acknowledge grants from the Canada Council Explorations Program, the Manitoba Arts Council, Manitoba Keewatinowi Okimakanak, Keewatin Tribal Council and the TARR Centre.

We thank all the Sayisi Dene who shared their memories with us. We thank Conrad Bjorklund and Christopher Anderson, who accompanied us on our pilgrimage to Dene Village.

The Assembly of Manitoba Chiefs paid for a visit to Kenora to the Anglican Church Archives, and let us use their computer to print some material while we were revising our first draft in a hotel room in Winnipeg. The Assembly of First Nations paid our hotel bills. Bruce Spence lent us his computer. Virginia Petch and Phil Dickman generously shared information.

We thank the staff at the University of Manitoba Press for the time and care they put into *Night Spirits,* and especially the Director, David Carr, for his thorough editorial attention and gracious support.

I would like to acknowledge my co-author, Üstün Bilgen-Reinart, whose encouragement, amazing perseverance, and hard work carried me through the pain of remembering many dark moments in my past, and who always managed to make me laugh and see the good side of life. My special appreciation goes to my husband, Ernie Bussidor, and to my sons, Jason and Dennis, and my daughters, Holly and Roseann, who are the centre of my life.

I am pleased to acknowledge the following organizations for their support in this project: the Assembly of First Nations, the Assembly of Manitoba Chiefs, the Keewatin Tribal Council, the Manitoba Keewatinowi Okimakanak, the Treaty and Aboriginal Rights Research Centre of Manitoba Inc., the Northwest Manitoba Community Futures Development Corporation, Calm Air International, Ltd., the Manitoba Arts Council, and the Canada Council.

A special thanks to Granny Betsy Anderson and to Elder Mary Sandberry. Thanks to Bruce Spence for his valuable advice, and to Geoffrey Bussidor for helping in the translation from Dene, and to those people who gave their time and patience in the interviews. I would also like to thank those who gave me their love and friendship, and who encouraged me not to give up on this book: my brothers and sisters — Sandy, Caroline, Tommy, Horace, Mary, Fred, Sarah, Sheila, and Little Peter; friends Belinda V., Ed A. and Theresa Y., Fred and Christine C., Jake and Margaret F., and Lorna M. My apologies to the many people I have missed.

I want to honour my people, the Sayisi Dene First Nation, and show my respect by honouring the spirits of my loved ones who are in the spirit world. I am extremely grateful to all. Ma See Cho.— Ila Bussidor

I warmly thank all my friends, especially Ann Atkey, Heather Frayne, Wanda Koop, and Susan Riley, who helped me at difficult moments. I also thank my husband, Jean Burelle, for his love and encouragement. — Üstün Bilgen-Reinart

INTRODUCTION

N*ight Spirits* tells the story of the Sayisi Dene, the story of their abrupt and tragic displacement in the mid-1950s, and their unspeakable suffering on the outskirts of Churchill, Manitoba. It is also the personal story of one of the Sayisi Dene, my friend Ila Bussidor. *Night Spirits* is told largely by Ila and the other Sayisi Dene, in their own voices.

For more than a thousand years, the Sayisi Dene had lived in what's now northern Manitoba and the Northwest Territories, between the open tundra and the tree line along the Churchill River. In fall, they hunted caribou. In winter, they moved south with the caribou herds. In summer they migrated north. They fished, gathered eggs, berries, and herbs. In the eighteenth century, the Hudson's Bay Company (HBC) began to draw them into the fur trade. By the twentieth century, trips to the trading post had become part of the Sayisi Dene's seasonal rounds. But they remained surprisingly independent, because the caribou provided for most of their needs.

In 1956, the Government of Canada moved the Sayisi Dene away from their traditional homeland and their way of life. The decision to "settle" the Sayisi Dene destroyed the independence of the hunters and trappers and turned them into slum dwellers in a frontier town, Churchill. They became broken and purposeless, with alcohol as their only solace. In fewer than ten years, their desolate settlement became a social wound, a place of grinding poverty, where people lived off the garbage dump and tore at each other in despair and rage. They had no control over the forces that were destroying them. They were despised by the townsfolk in Churchill. Many of them died sudden, unnatural deaths.

In the early 1970s, about 300 survivors, deeply wounded from the degradation that destroyed their people, returned to the wilderness, to the shores of Tadoule Lake, 250 kilometres west of Churchill, and they set up a new community. But the wilderness survival skills that they had acquired through hundreds of years and passed on from generation to generation were lost. The Sayisi Dene's finely tuned connection to the cycles of nature was cut. Their wounds festered.

Like all Aboriginal peoples in Manitoba, the Sayisi Dene are now at a crossroads. After having been governed by the federal Department of Indian Affairs for close to a century, in 1995 they began to run their own health, education, and community programs. Ila and others in her community at Tadoule Lake are telling their story at this crucial juncture, because they believe that knowing about the past can help shape the future.

Ila Bussidor and I met in February 1985, when I was a current-affairs reporter for CBC-TV in Winnipeg. The principal of the primary school at Tadoule Lake had called me to suggest that I do a story about the unique community where the people were gradually rebuilding their lives in the northern wilderness.

A couple of weeks after that phone call, I got on a Calm Air flight out of Thompson to Tadoule Lake. The twin-engine Beaver landed on the frozen lake at noon. I stood beside the plane, blinking in the blinding glare, with tiny icicles on my eyelashes. I had never been so far north before. I was astonished at the beauty of the place. The cold air was perfumed with spruce and wood smoke. A white light rose from the vast, snow-covered lake. The spruce forest loomed on the far shore. A fishing boat lay upside down on the beach. An esker (a sand hill left behind from an ancient glacier) rose beyond the beach, and log cabins were scattered here and there, beside teepees used for smoking fish and meat. Laundry, frozen stiff, moved in the wind.

Dozens of snowmobiles suddenly appeared on the horizon and converged beside the plane from all directions, their riders covered in dark snowmobile suits and goggles. One of them took me into the settlement.

I stayed at the nursing station, the newest building in the community and the only one with running water. It was empty most of the time because a doctor flew in to the community only once a week. I had brought my own food for ten days.

Tadoule Lake was a "dry" community. Volunteer constable Isaac Thom boasted,

"No alcohol, no violence." He told me that, since there was no violence to deal with, he passed his time carrying water to the elders who needed help. In one of the cabins, an older woman was hanging slabs of caribou meat to dry on a wooden rack above a woodstove. In another cabin, a woman was scraping caribou hide with a tool made of bone, just as her mother and her grandmother had done. An elderly man, Thomas Duck, agreed to take me out to his trap line. We set out at dawn for a three-hour snowmobile ride. (It was the coldest I've ever been in my life, despite the fact that Thomas's niece, Edith Duck, had lent me her snowmobile suit and her caribou-hide boots.) At lunch time, Thomas melted some snow to make us tea, and he offered me and the cameraman dried meat and bannock. As we warmed up with the steaming tea, life seemed idyllic.

The band organized a drum dance during my visit. In the circle of people stepping to the syncopated beat, there were elders, young people, and children. I noticed the absence of middle-aged people. "They're dead," Chief Peter Yassie told me later. An entire generation — close to 100 people — had perished in Churchill. "There's no one left to teach our children traditional skills," he said. "How will they face the future?"

Many young people were leaving Tadoule Lake because they didn't know how to survive in the wilderness, and because there were no jobs in the settlement. One of those people was Ila Bussidor, who had become a trainee in the Native Communications program in Thompson, Manitoba. Someone gave me her address. On my way back from Tadoule Lake to Winnipeg, I visited Ila in her modern suburban apartment in Thompson. During our interview, she told me she was sad to leave Tadoule Lake, but she wanted to study and to work.

Ila and I met again in 1988. By this time she had become the chief of the Fort Churchill Sayisi Dene Band. As chief, she had travelled to a meeting of the Assembly of First Nations in Quebec City, and she had attracted national attention with an impassioned presentation to the minister of Indian Affairs about the injuries inflicted on her people. We became friends around that time.

In 1990, when Ila was pregnant with her third child, she resigned as chief. Around that time, she told me she wanted to tell her story, and the story of her people, in a book. She wanted me to do it with her. She wanted us to record the memories of surviving Sayisi Dene elders. Her own granny was in her nineties — she remembered life before the treaties, she knew the old legends. I encouraged Ila to write the book alone, to start by talking into a tape recorder. In the spring of 1994, she came right out and asked me to begin to work with her, and I realized she meant business. My first impulse was to pull back. I knew about some of the heart-breaking injuries my friend and her people had suffered. But to enter their experience, to re-live those nightmares with Ila, and to navigate a joint project with her, seemed perilous.

But when Ila decides to do something, she does not take no for an answer. She told me simply that we were meant to write this book together.

I flew back to Tadoule Lake in mid-October of 1994, nine years after my first visit. At first glance, the esker on the shores of the lake and the charcoal shadows of spruce on the far shore still looked idyllic. The October sky put on a light show in the afternoon when gold streaks broke through gray and mauve clouds. Smoke was rising from the chimneys of the pre-fabricated houses that had replaced the log cabins on the slope rising to the esker.

Ila and Ernie Bussidor's three-bedroom house was on the south shore of the lake. With a woodstove roaring and hissing at the centre of the house and large windows looking out onto the lake, it felt like a resort cottage. On the afternoon of my arrival, Ila and I headed to the one-room cabin of Ila's almost 100-year-old granny, Betsy Anderson. The sky was steely gray, with crimson streaks to the west. The air smelt of wood smoke as it always does in fall and winter at Tadoule Lake. The wind carried a powdery snow.

Inside, a kettle was boiling on the woodstove, the steam rising from its spout fogging the windows. We put our tape recorder on the little table beside the bed, and Ila began the interview. They spoke in Dene. Granny Betsy's low, raspy voice rose slowly, deliberately, between coughing spells. She smoked. And she laughed every once in a while, a gleeful cackle. Hours passed; the room became dark and filled with smoke.

The next day we returned. Again, outside, the sky turned crimson and the room grew dark with shadows, and Granny Betsy talked about what she had lived, what she had seen, what she had lost.

The next day, and the day after, and the day after that, it was Ila who did the talking into the tape recorder. For hours and hours, she re-lived the years in Church-ill. We had closeted ourselves in the one-room ATCO trailer that served as the resource classroom of the local school. Ila's older sister Sarah Cheekie came into that trailer too, eager to tell her story.

Sarah had been among the handful of Sayisi Dene teenagers who had made it to university, but she had dropped out because her life was too chaotic. She was now working for the band on a program called Brighter Futures Initiative, which was set up to encourage young people to produce art as a healing tool. She'd had alcohol problems almost all her life. Ten years before, her drinking was so bad that her two children were apprehended. She fought to get them back and she fought to control her drinking.

Sarah began to sob as she told us about the night of the fire that had killed their parents. She described how she had run into the burning house and heard her mother crying, how she had woken up in a hospital bed the next morning to learn that her parents were dead. "No matter how much I drank, I couldn't get that sound out of my ears," she said, shaking with sobs, "the sound of my drunk mother crying in the burning house." Sarah and Ila held each other and cried together for a long time.

On most evenings, elderly men played cards in the band hall. One of them, Ronnie John Bussidor, told us how he had helped to get the people out of Churchill and back to the land twenty-seven years before. Ronnie had never lost his knowledge of the land because he had stayed in North River while everyone else was living in Churchill. Now, in his seventies, he lamented his loneliness. "Long ago, our grandfathers predicted this would come about," he said, "that our people would speak another language, and that they would lose connection with the ways of the Sayisi Dene."

On Tuesday evening, there was a light on over the door of the Sayisi Dene band hall, and a steady stream of people were filing in. It was the night for bingo, the most popular social event in Tadoule Lake. Granny Betsy slowly walked up the slope to the hall, her colourful scarf tied under her chin, her back hunched over her walking stick. After settling at a table near the door and spreading her bingo sheets and bingo dabber in front of her, she waved at Ila, who had settled at the far corner of the hall. As the bingo caller announced the numbers, Ila whispered to me, giggling, "My granny plays bingo without glasses. That's something she's proud of."

The next morning, Ila was doing laundry — a thankless and endless task in the absence of running water and an automatic washer. She heated water, poured it in an old-fashioned machine, then emptied it out before re-filling the machine for the next load. She was worried about her sixteen-year-old son, Jason, who was supposed to be going to high school in Thompson, but who had been arrested twice for drinking under age. The school was threatening to expel him. "He hangs out with a gang. I'm afraid they'll get into real trouble. They could get into drugs or into fights with other gangs."

Jason is the oldest of Ila and Ernie's four children. The second oldest is Holly, Ila's helper and confidante. Holly was twelve in 1994. After school, Holly frequently baby-sat for the two younger ones: four-year-old Dennis and three-year-old Rosie.

In 1994, Ila's husband, Ernie, was the chief of the Fort Churchill Sayisi Dene band at Tadoule Lake. Ernie had never known the "white" American soldier who had fathered him in Churchill in 1956 (the year when the Sayisi Dene were moved to Churchill). His mother, Mina Jones, was one of the most beautiful girls in the community — she eventually gave birth to eight children from four different men, three of whom were "white" and all of whom abandoned her. Ernie was raised by Mina's parents. He is an attractive, articulate man, with a gentle manner and a shy smile, but he lives with what he calls demons — angry outbursts that bewilder him and injure the people he loves. "I've treated Ila the way I saw adults around me treat their partners when I was a kid. I treated her as a possession. I am sorry that Jason grew up in an environment where I was totally unable to understand what was wrong."

Soon, I saw that violence was a part of the lives of many families in Tadoule Lake. One morning, while I was waiting at the check-out counter of the Dene Trading Post (the only store in Tadoule Lake), I saw a young woman buying cigarettes who had big black bruises near her eyes. I'd heard that another young woman had recently had to be escorted away from Tadoule Lake to a hospital in Thompson after being beaten so badly that she could hardly open her eyes.

Ila called it "a disease." "When people start to heal, we'll learn to live together without violence," she said. "Until then, our kids will suffer too. I already see it in my children. If I don't try to heal myself, I'm no good to my children. I can't help them. I see Jason going through a tough time trying to grow up. I know that what he has seen between me and Ernie in his sixteen short years has damaged him. I have to think about how I can help myself so that I can help others."

When we began to interview people, Ila told me she was worried that I was going to be shocked by the way things had been at Churchill. She kept saying life had been "too ugly." As we listened to people's memories, I understood what she meant. The world that emerged as Sayisi Dene survivors described their Churchill years was so dark as to be unbearable. I took walks along the lake, listening to the lapping of the water, and reminding myself that Ila's determination to tell this story was an act of hope.

By the end of that first week of interviewing, Ila was exhausted. Later, she told me she had felt depressed after I left because we had re-awakened too many painful memories. But she continued to do interviews in Dene. She interviewed other elders, she taped her older sister and brothers, and she transcribed and translated those interviews.

Ila had agreed to go to Churchill with me, to complete our research. If the week-long re-living of the past had been hard, the trip to Churchill with me was going to be harder. Ila dreaded the trip. She was tense and edgy as we made our travel arrangements. "I know I have unfinished business there," she told me.

Blowing snow slapped our faces as soon as we walked out of the plane in Churchill in the early afternoon. The November sky hung gray and low over the tree-less horizon, as if no light could break through the dense clouds. Over the bay, enormous charcoal waves broke on black boulders, raising a white spray. Snowbanks rose like abstract sculptures on the barren land. Pre-fabricated buildings with small windows huddled on the side of the road, their entrances facing away from the ocean where ice was just beginning to form. Churchill's landmark, the enormous grain elevator, rose in the distance like some ancient monument, lifeless in the forbidding landscape.

It was mid-afternoon when we checked into our room at the Seaport Hotel; the sky was already turning dark. Ila stood at the window and said:

See that corner? That lamppost in front of the Northern Store? I used to stand on that corner with my mom at Christmas time when she was trying to sell beaded moccasins and mitts. . . . One year, we were standing there. I was about ten years old. There were all these shoppers going back and forth. It was already dark. The shops were going to close soon. It was snowing. I was raising my face up, sticking my tongue out and looking up at the big white flakes fluttering down in the light of the street lamp. The snowflakes were falling on my tongue. What if we had a dollar for every snowflake that's falling, I was thinking. I thought that because we needed money. My mom was a little shy, reluctant to approach people to say, "Do you want to buy this?" Maybe she was scared of being turned down. "Ask this person," she would say to me in Dene, and I would approach that person and say, "Do you want to buy a pair of mitts or slippers?"

We stared out the window at the corner of Kelsey Boulevard and Hudson Square, at the yellowish light the street light shed on the blowing snow. A pickup truck slowed down under the light, spinning its wheels. It lurched forward and disappeared around the corner.

Overnight, the gray waves of Hudson Bay were replaced by slabs of ice. In the morning, we were to drive out to Dene Village, the site of the notorious settlement where the Sayisi Dene lived and died in squalor during the late sixties. We rented a four-wheel-drive truck because the snow was deep, and the drifts were treacherous. Ila insisted we needed someone to go with us to Dene Village. She saw menace and evil everywhere. It was not safe to go there alone. No. There are polar bears. There are snow drifts. There are spirits.

A couple of hours later, we were on our way with not one, but two, young men — Christopher and Conrad, sons of Sayisi Dene women Ila knew from her days in Dene Village. On the way, I wanted to keep silent and to absorb what I was about to see. To my surprise, Ila was talking a steady stream.

The flat land stretched on, beyond both sides of the road, white as far as the eye could see, marked only by the black steel lines of the railway tracks. We passed two gray buildings of the former navy base — now vacant, black holes gaping through their broken windows. About seven kilometres southeast of Churchill, the road forked. We turned right, away from the main highway leading to the airport. Several hundred metres further on, we approached something unusual around Churchill: a cluster of thin black spruce, stunted by the relentless wind.

The truck slowed down in the snow as we turned off the road onto a lane winding between the trees. Near the corner, there was a square-shaped cement outline on the ground. "That was Peter Yassie's house," Ila said. "It burned down with three children in it." As we slowly drove through the lane, we could see rows of similar concrete squares on both sides: three-foot-high cement foundations, the remains of the houses in Dene Village.

Ila refused to get out of the truck; she said lingering spirits made her sad. I left her there, in the safety of conversation, and I stepped out to walk in the knee-deep snow. The sky was heavy. The wind howled in the branches of the scraggly black spruce.

The lane that had been the main road through the community was now empty. I walked between the dry willow bushes towards the cement square that had once been the foundation of a small, draughty house. I stood there and listened to the wind. I was holding my breath, trying to move silently. I was on sacred ground.

I crossed the lane to get to the remains of the home of Ila's parents, Artie and Suzanna Cheekie: a square-shaped cement foundation just like the others. Dry weeds sticking out of the clean, new snow fluttered in the wind. As I quietly gazed around the foundation, I saw something that made me freeze: a piece of charred beam still attached to the cement, its black stubby end sticking out of the snow — the only evidence of the fire that had destroyed the house.

Just a few metres behind the remains of the house, on the other side of a stubby willow bush, the railway tracks stretched into the distance. People had told me about frozen bodies found at those tracks. Ila had told me she had come home one day and found her mother lying beside the tracks, crying. I stared at those steel lines surrounded by black trees, snow, and the gray sky. I turned towards the south: nothing but black spruce and railway tracks in the snow. I turned north: two parallel black lines leading to a vast, snow-filled horizon and a dark sky, beautiful in its indifference.

I closed my eyes and imagined human shapes slumped in the snow. In my mind's eye, someone stumbled and fell in a heap along the railroad while the snow kept blowing. I heard moans, screams, whispers, and a howling wind. In a January blizzard, were there children huddling inside these concrete walls? Was it on this lane that mobs of boys tormented drunk women? And was it right here that Ila's mother, Suzanna Cheekie, lay weeping one summer afternoon in 1971, grieving over her wasted life, mourning her own approaching death? Now, Dene Village was empty of human sounds. The gray sky, the black spruce and the damp wind together sang an endless dirge over its cement remains.

We are telling this story to honour the memory of Ila's parents, Suzanna and Artie Cheekie, to honour the memories of all who perished in Churchill. We also want to honour those who were humiliated and injured in Churchill, those who today live in pain and in shame and who have to move forward somehow because there is no going back. Before healing can begin, the injury has to be described. This is a dark story. We're telling it in hope.

Üstün Bilgen-Reinart

The Narrators of This Book

Most of this story is told by the Sayisi Dene themselves, in their own words. They were interviewed by Üstün Bilgen-Reinart and Ila Bussidor between October 1994 and February 1996. Many of the older Dene, including Betsy Anderson, spoke in their own language; their interviews were translated by Ila Bussidor. The excerpts from interviews with Stewart Yassie and Jimmy Clipping are taken from interviews that are part of a study of the relocation commissioned in 1996 by the Sayisi Dene First Nation.

Also interviewed were Phil Dickman and Martha Commodore, who worked with the Sayisi Dene at Churchill; Dolores MacFarlane; and Virginia Petch, who prepared a background report on the Sayisi Dene for the Royal Commission on Aboriginal Peoples.

Along with Ila and Ernie Bussidor and Betsy Anderson, the Sayisi Dene whose voices make up most of this book are:

EVA ANDERSON, a Dene elder who lived in Duck Lake and Churchill. Eva Anderson was Eva Yassie's grandmother. She passed away in 1995.
CAROLINE BJORKLUND, a Sayisi Dene who married a Métis man and returned to work as a teacher's aide at Churchill in 1967.

RONNIE JOHN BUSSIDOR, who grew up in Duck Lake and who was thirty years old when the 1956 relocation took place.

SARAH CHEEKIE, Ila Bussidor's sister.

CHARLIE KITHITHEE, who grew up and lived in the Sayisi Dene community of North River. He was twenty years old in 1956.

JOHN SOLOMON, who was thirty years old in 1956 and lived in Duck Lake.

CAROLINE YASSIE, Ila Bussidor's older sister.

EVA YASSIE, who, like Ila and Ernie Bussidor, grew up in Camp-10 and Dene Village.

MARY (MOWATT) YASSIE, who lived in Camp-10 and Dene Village. She is married to Eva Anderson's grandson Fred.

RUBINA YASSIE, who was in her late twenties during the relocation. She is the daughter of Betsy Anderson.

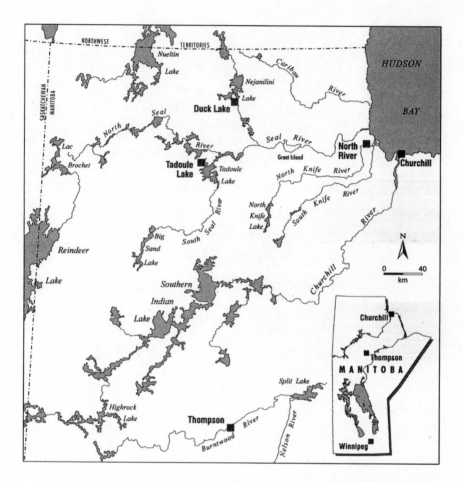

Northern Manitoba

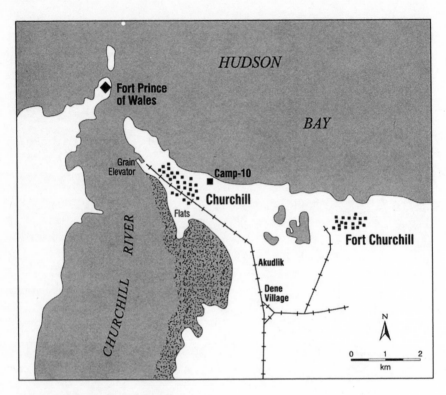

Churchill, Manitoba, c. 1967

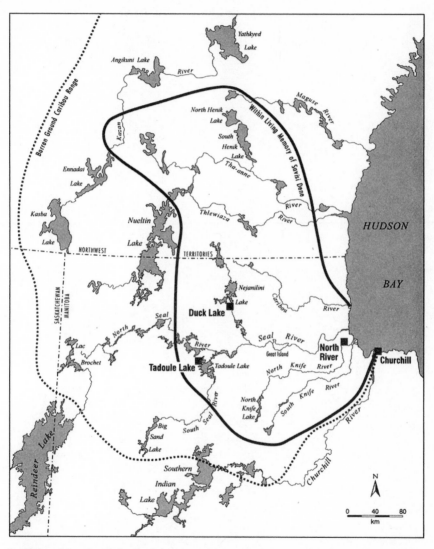

Traditional Lands of the Sayisi Dene Based on "Within Living Memory" Land Use
(modified from Petch, "Relocation," figure 1, page 2.)

(above) Sayisi Dene family at Churchill, Manitoba, 1894 *(HBCA)*

(right) Chief and councillors, Fort Churchill Chipewyan Band (Sayisi Dene First Nation), after the signing of the adhesion to Treaty Five at Fort Prince of Wales, 1910 *(PAM, A.V. Thomas collection)*

(top) A group of Sayisi Dene preparing to go north, Caribou Post, Christmas, c. 1932-34 *(HBCA)*

(above) John Duck and John Bussidor with their children, Caribou Post, 1935 *(HBCA)*

(right) John and Mary Ann Thorassie and family, Duck Lake, 1947 *(HBCA)*

(left top) Sayisi Dene camps,
Duck Lake, c. 1950
(R.C. Diocese of Churchill)

(left bottom) Sayisi Dene during
the visit of Bishop Hives to
Duck Lake, c. 1954. The tall
man at the left is Artie Cheekie,
Ila Bussidor's father. The boy
with the cap is Jimmy Clipping.
(Anglican Diocese of Keewatin)

(top) Alice Solomon, Duck Lake,
1952 *(HBCA)*

(bottom) The carcasses of caribou
after the fall hunt, Duck Lake,
1952. This is one of the photographs used by game officials
and conservationists to argue
against the Dene caribou hunt.
(HBCA)

(above) A view
of Camp-10 from the
Churchill cemetery, 1966.
Hudson Bay is in the
background.

(opposite bottom) Suzanna
Cheekie with her children,
North River, 1957

(above) Camp-10, with
Hudson Bay in the back-
ground, 1966

(opposite top) Dene Village, 1968

(opposite bottom) Dene Village, 1968

(above) Dene Village, Treaty Day, 1968. The man with the sunglasses is Artie Cheekie.

(above) Tadoule Lake,
c. 1985

(opposite bottom)Lyle
Wasteste, Sarah Cheekie,
Marjorie Cheekie, Fred
Cheekie, Tadoule Lake,
c. 1976

(left) Eva Anderson, Tadoule
Lake, c. 1989

(above) Traditional Dene hand game, Tadoule Lake, c. 1988. Counterclockwise from top left: Ernie Bussidor, Jimmy Clipping, Jimmy Ellis, Thomas Cutlip, Tony Duck, Alex Sandberry, and Thomas Duck.

(left) Ila Bussidor and Betsy Anderson, Tadoule Lake, 1994

Night Spirits

MY STORY

This is the story of my family and my people. I want to share the memories and the traumas of my childhood with you. I want to tell you about the loving memories of my mother and my father before they were destroyed by what we call "fire-water" in my native tongue, Sayisi Dene. I want to go back to when I was a little girl and re-live the time when my father would come home from his trap line and lift me up in his big, strong arms, kiss me, and swing me up in the air. I want to feel again my mother's tenderness as she cared for me and my brothers and sisters. I want to feel her arms around me as she rocked me back and forth, softly singing a lullaby in Dene. I felt safe, very loved, and protected then.

My parents belonged to a traditional generation of the Sayisi Dene. They were once untouched by the white man's poison, fire-water. They were both fluent in Dene; they didn't speak or read the white man's language. From my grandparents, they had learned well the skills of living off the land, in the same way that hundreds of generations had done before them.

That gift of survival, that gift of traditional skills passed from generation to generation, would stop suddenly. It was a gift that would never be given to me and my brothers and sisters, because in 1956, the Government of Canada relocated my people from our homeland. We were left on the fringes of a frontier town, Churchill, Manitoba. For us, that is when the nightmare began.

The Sayisi Dene were skilled hunters. We could live off the land and move with the great caribou herds that provided everything we needed to survive. Life was simple and complete. My parents were among these people. But, when the Government of Canada moved my people from Duck Lake, they left us with welfare vouchers and macaroni rations. This move destroyed our traditional livelihood, our culture, and our language. Our land was no longer ours to harvest as we had done for centuries. It is sad, but if it had not been for the garbage dump, I am sure that many of my generation would have starved to death in Churchill during those years.

In the Dene Nation, my people are known as "the Sayisi" — the Dene from the east. We possess a history as rich and as vast as the land we inhabit. We are descendants of great, historic leaders like Mattonabee and Bekkenshies. In the eyes of the Creator, we were no different from the caribou. We moved and lived with the herds, and loved the beauty of the wide-open tundra and the bounty of our land. We were nomadic by tradition and of necessity throughout the ages, but we finally yielded to sign Treaty Five in 1910. We attempted to make a stationary life at Duck Lake, where a Hudson's Bay Company post was located. Some of our clans established smaller settlements at nearby North River and Caribou Lake. It was to have been, and should have been, a gradual adaptation to an inevitable way of living. The adaptation to stationary living needed time and patience to work.

Instead, in 1956, we were airlifted off the land and left on the banks of the Churchill River. For the Sayisi Dene, this arbitrary government decision brought culture shock, disorientation and confusion. For my people, it was the beginning of two decades of destruction and suffering. During our time at Churchill, nearly a third of the Sayisi Dene perished — many from alcohol abuse and violence. For my people, the impact of the relocation had the same effect as genocide.

I was born during that time, when the Sayisi Dene were stripped of everything they stood for as a people. I grew up surrounded by the destruction of alcohol. We lived in a slum in total darkness. As a child, I learned what it felt like to be inferior to another race, to be less than the next person because I was Dene. Because of the racism we faced every day, I was ashamed to be Dene. I wished I belonged to another race of people. I thought anything was better than being a Sayisi Dene. I learned to be afraid and I knew what hunger pangs were. Cupboards in most homes were always empty and children were hungry the majority of the time. I was one of them. As a young child, I already knew what it felt like to be desperate and without hope. I learned what it felt like to have no hope, to be desperate. At the same time, I had also been given something that was unspeakably beautiful — the love that my parents had given me from the day I was born until the time they started drinking. I knew what it was like to be loved and to love deeply.

I loved my parents, my sisters, and my brothers. When you love deeply, you may know deep sorrow too. I watched my parents become broken people and die tragically. I witnessed the burning of our house, while they were trapped inside, drunk. When they died, a big part of my spirit died with them.

I remember watching other house fires. People died in all of them. My memories of this time are filled with sadness. I know my spirit was injured by the tragic deaths, by alcohol and drug abuse, by violence, from being sexually abused by drunken men.

And I wasn't the only person who suffered these injuries. All Sayisi Dene, especially those of my generation, have a personal account of brutal hardship and despair. We were terribly hurt by this ordeal. As children, we watched as our parents were destroyed, unable to bear the weight of a way of life that did not belong to them. We witnessed people being beaten, murdered, people of all ages dying in house fires, young women and girls being raped and beaten. Men and women froze to death every winter; there were countless victims of hit-and-run accidents.

In Churchill, we were reduced to humiliation. We were victims of cruel discrimination from other ethnic groups — the whites, the Inuit, the Métis and the Cree. As children, we believed at an early age that we were not Indians — we felt we were lower than that. We came to believe that we were the last Dene people in the world.

The pain from the relocation stays with us, no matter how hard we try to go forward. The damage is something we may never repair — as is evident in my community today. I am left with scars that will remain with me for the rest of my life, just like everyone who lived through and survived that nightmare. We need to heal ourselves as a people.

Now that I'm older and have my own family, I realize that I have nothing to be ashamed of. I know now that, before the relocation, my parents were proud and dignified, that they were skilled people like all the Sayisi Dene. For hundreds of years my people had been hunters. They hunted the great caribou herds that have always been at the heart of my people. When the government forced this relocation on us, our survival skills fell apart. Everything that happened in that time to the Sayisi Dene was unjust. It was wrong that any people were made to live and die through what my people experienced. We were normal people, caught in a horrible situation, which we had no control over.

Most Canadians do not know that during the 1960s and 1970s, when Canada was booming, building, and inventing, my people were caught in this nightmare. Along with our independence, our innocence, and many lives, we lost immeasurable potential. We lost the potential of generations of children yet to be born, and the knowledge of our elders and parents, who took their wisdom with them when they died in Churchill.

It is sad that we did not have the skills, knowledge, and resources to speak for ourselves during those terrible years. When I was a young girl, I often wished I could help my parents, although I did not fully understand something that I could feel was so wrong. I wondered, How can I make something right out of a terrible situation? Telling my story now might correct some of the outsiders' misconceptions about my people. Our story may show the government what a terrible mistake they made when they uprooted my people.

I tell this story for my mother and my father, who I know are with me in spirit. I know that they would be proud of me if they were alive. I live today to complete a task that they were unable to accomplish because they were weakened by the loss of their way of life.

In many ways, I have followed in their footsteps. My father was one of the leaders in his time. Many years before the relocation, before alcohol took control of his life, he was the chief of our people. Years later, I too was elected chief and served my people as the first woman chief in the history of the Sayisi Dene. It took me a long time to realize that my parents had given me some important principles for life. They had left me with vision and hope. I am the mother of four children. From my mother, I have inherited the ability to love and care for my children. Like her, I have the ability to be strong throughout the worst storms that life can bring. I have inherited her set of principles about right and wrong. I know that the spirits of my parents have continued to care for me and guide me even after their deaths. For this reason I am speaking out today to share what I know.

One spring day, when I was ten or eleven years old, I went to the town dump in Churchill with some neighbours and carried home food scraps in a little box tied on my back. There was nothing unusual about this. All of us went to the dump to look for food. But that day, when I came home and put the box on the table, my father stood near the window of our house. He was crying. As he stood there, he turned towards my mother and said, "I was once a leader for my people and my children. I stood tall and walked with pride and dignity. My people and my children never went hungry. When my family needed food, all I had to do was to go out on our land and hunt. I never came home empty-handed. The clothes I wore were the best — beaded caribou-hide jackets, beaded mukluks, and gloves. I would never wear anything that was torn or even a little ripped. That is how proud I was. I had the confidence and respect of my people. Now, look at my baby daughter, bringing food thrown away by other people, so that I can eat." When he said this, I couldn't understand what he meant. I was too young. All I knew was that I loved my father and that it made me sad to see him cry.

I will never forget how my father lifted me in his arms and sobbed that day. That memory came back to me with a great force twenty years later, when I was chief and was standing at a microphone to make a presentation to the minister of Indian Affairs at a national chiefs' conference. Suddenly, I understood what my father had meant on that spring day in Churchill. I understood how it must have broken him as a man, as a leader, and above all as a father. I understood his burden and his shame. It was as if he were there and I was speaking for him. I broke down and cried when I thought about Holly, my daughter. I would rather die than see her scrounge for food in the dump.

There was a time when the Sayisi Dene men made their annual trip from Duck Lake to Churchill with their furs just before Christmas. They were dressed so well in traditional clothes, in beaded jackets trimmed with wolf or fox fur, with beaded gloves and mukluks. Their sleds were so well-made, and decorated so beautifully with ribbons and with bells, that they were the envy of outsiders. Those men had hope for their people and their children. My father was one of them. In ten short years, that hope was crushed out of them.

During the 1960s and the 1970s, most of the people in Churchill despised the Dene. We were thought of as drunks. We were in and out of jails. Our children and youths would run around all hours of the night, breaking into stores and stealing whatever they could. There was violence and neglect everywhere. How ignorant were those people? Didn't they realize that the Sayisi Dene had been competent enough to live in one of the harshest environments in the world, that at a moment's notice, the whole community could move to follow a caribou herd in the dead of winter? Did no one see how tragic it was that men like my father — in the prime of their lives, men who had once stood on top of the world — had now sunk so low? Didn't anyone in that town see that these people hadn't been drunk all their lives?

They said we were useless, drunken, lazy Indians. That there was no hope for us. That's what made me so ashamed to be Dene when I was a child. I did not know the history of my people as I do today. I want my daughter Holly to know that history and to never be ashamed that she is a Sayisi Dene.

Today, as we approach the twenty-first century, we face contradictions and challenges. We have a lot of catching up to do. At a time when my people should have been negotiating with the federal government, we were living in a slum. No one consulted us before sectioning off a big part of our territory for the Nunavut land-claim settlement between the Inuit and the federal government. This was another injustice done to the Sayisi Dene.

After leaving Churchill, my people slowly drifted together at Tadoule Lake, and, from the fragments, in 1973 we came to be a community of people again. We are now connected to the outside world through a computer system and satellite TV, but we live without running water or sanitation. No roads lead into our community. Tadoule Lake is now over twenty years old, but there is still a feeling of emptiness in our hearts. Many of the generation of people that we needed to teach us the Dene way died in Churchill. The older people who are alive today have never fully recovered from the ordeal of the relocation. Without them, we are alone to rediscover our traditions and to rebuild our culture.

But today we slowly are reviving our traditional drum songs, drum dances, and feasts. We are teaching our language at our school. As we gradually take control of our own health, education, and social programs, we turn to our traditional culture for strength and for pride.

In this story, I want to tell you some beautiful memories that live in me, and also the many sad ones of physical and sexual abuse that took place in what was called "Dene Village," probably one of the worst slums in Manitoba's history. As a young girl growing up to become a woman, I also abused the poison fire-water. I sank to depths of misery and shame, close to death, many, many times. Today, the generations of Sayisi Dene that survived the relocation still struggle with alcohol and drug addiction, and I am no exception.

As a survivor of the Churchill years, by telling the true story of my people and my family, I am beginning a journey that's very important for my life and for my children. This is a good day to begin to travel the road towards healing. My spirit is allowing me to be free and not to be afraid to stand in my truth.

Maybe today my story will help some young Native person experiencing hardship, someone the same age as I was when my people lived in Churchill, to reach deep within herself and realize that, no matter how hard life can be, there is courage and strength that lies within each and every one of us. It's just a matter of looking within; everything we need is there. Listen to what your spirit tells you. You must believe in yourself. Perhaps it will strengthen children like my own.

May this story be a living monument to our relatives who lost their lives to the Churchill relocation. Every story is a tool we can use if we want to. That is what our elders say. Ma See Cho.

Ila Bussidor
Sayisi Dene First Nation
Tadoule Lake, Manitoba

The Caribou and the People

BETSY ANDERSON

There was a time when all the people and all the animals understood each other and spoke the same language. The story I'm telling you is about that time.

They say the caribou left the land and went back in the ground. The people travelled all over the land, as far as they could go, and still they couldn't see where the caribou had gone to. They made a necklace made of caribou eyes and put it around a raven's neck. They let the raven fly away, hoping that it would find the caribou and lead the people to the herd. But the raven disappeared.

Just then, another bird landed beside the people, a small eagle. He said, "I'll watch where the raven is going to. If my vision becomes blurred, wave an object in front of my eyes so I can see far away into the distance." The people kept waving a stick in front of the eagle's eyes and the small eagle saw the raven. The raven had found the caribou but he was keeping the herd captive underground, in a vast cave.

The cave's entrance was covered with a curtain made of caribou organs: stomach linings and hearts. In front of that strange curtain, hungry foxes were jumping up and down, trying to grab some of that organ meat. The raven was swooping down upon them trying to protect the entrance to the cave. But the foxes managed to break a hole in the covering of the entrance, and suddenly the caribou started to stampede out. Soon, thousands of caribou covered the land, their antlers filled the horizon. The caribou spread across this land of ours for our people to hunt and live on.

One year, there was a lot of caribou everywhere. The people had lots to eat, and lots of hide to keep them warm. A young Sayisi Dene woman walked up to one of the caribou and tagged it on the ear with a piece of hide dyed with berries. "Next year when the caribou come back," she said, "I'll know that this one is mine. I'll be able to identify it because my tag will be on its ear." But the caribou were offended. It wasn't right for somebody to claim ownership of any animal in the herd. They decided to go away.

Next year, people kept looking for signs of the caribou, but they saw none. All over the land, the Dene were starving. Their clothes made of caribou hide became tattered. The caribou stayed away. This went on for years.

Finally, some medicine men got together to figure out a way to find the caribou and to make them return. One of the medicine men set out on a long journey to look for the caribou. He travelled far away. Other animals helped him along the way. A loon and a swan helped him cross a big lake. At long last he found the caribou herd. He transformed himself into a warble fly and he crawled under the skin of the caribou, near his ear. He talked to the animal who was the leader of the herd. "My people are starving," he said. "We need you to come back."

The caribou agreed to return — but on one condition. "As long as the people live and as long as you depend on us," said the caribou, "don't ever allow anyone to claim ownership of us again." The young girl who had tagged the caribou had to remove that tag and ask for forgiveness. The caribou roamed free after that. They were there when the people needed them.

The People from the East

From time immemorial, the Sayisi Dene have lived on the land to the west of Hudson Bay, where the boreal forest meets the barren grounds. Their traditional homeland covered a vast territory that straddled the present-day border between northern Manitoba and the Northwest Territories.[1]

The vast sub-arctic region extending north and west from Hudson Bay, all the way to the Mackenzie Valley and to the Great Bear and Great Slave Lakes, was home to more than twenty related but distinct Dene peoples, all of whom spoke an Athapaskan language.[2] The Sayisi Dene lived on the eastern edge of that wide and varied Dene world, and that's why they called themselves *Sayisi*, "the people from the east."

Anthropologists used the term *Caribou eaters* (*Edthen-eldili-dene*) to describe all Dene peoples who lived in the northern woodlands, including the Sayisi Dene. To the early fur traders of the HBC, they were simply Northern Indians. But, by the twentieth century, many Dene people, including the Sayisi, were known as Chipewyan, a Cree word meaning "pointed skins," probably describing the caribou-hide coats the Dene wore in winter.

The elders say that the Sayisi Dene were once "like the trees in a forest" — there were thousands of them on that permanently frozen land where the wind stunts the spruce, the tamarack, and the dwarf willow, and where the tree line gives way to vast expanses of rocky ground covered by moss.

They followed the migratory movements of the great caribou herds. In the spring, the herds would move north to the barren grounds for calving. The Sayisi Dene also moved north to spend the summer in the land east of Great Slave Lake, where they fished and picked berries and herbs. In the fall, the caribou would turn south again, moving towards the relative shelter of the forests.[3]

As thousands of caribou made their great trek south, the Sayisi Dene would hunt them. A group of hunters would set up camp near a body of water they knew to be a caribou crossing. Sometimes they would build "pounds" from bushy branches of trees and would lead the herd into a pound and snare the animals there. Sometimes they would wait for the herd to swim across the lake (or the river) and would set out in canoes and spear the animals.[4] They killed as many as they could. After the kill, they carefully skinned some of the carcasses and took them to their campsites for immediate use, but they left most of them on the shore, in heaps, for use during the brutal winter. Snow would cover the carcasses and keep them in a deep freeze. At times of need, people could find the meat by poking long, thin sticks into the snow.

The Sayisi Dene wasted no part of the caribou. The women dried and smoked the meat. They used the fat for cooking and for lanterns. They made clothes, snowshoes, and teepees from the hide, using sinews as thread. Caribou bones served as their tools.

As they moved between the taiga and the tundra, the Sayisi Dene occasionally came across other Aboriginal peoples. The Churchill River and related lakes formed a natural boundary between them and the Cree. The Great Slave Lake to the west separated them from other Dene peoples. Further north along the coastal waters of Hudson Bay were the Inuit.

No one knows what kind of relationship the different Aboriginal peoples had with each other before the arrival of the Europeans, because there are no records of their history. In the seventeenth century, the British set up the HBC and began to establish posts along the Hudson Bay coast to trade with the Cree. Within a few years, the region was convulsed in violence and bloodshed. The Europeans attracted the Cree near York Factory to the fur trade by offering them household goods and guns. Guns gave the Cree great power in the North. They began to act as middlemen and to collect furs from other Aboriginal groups. They wanted to prevent other Aboriginal peoples from trading directly with the Europeans.[5]

In 1717, the HBC established a trading post in Churchill, on the southwestern shore of Hudson Bay, to attract the Northern Indians to the fur trade. The

Company built a wooden fort on the western shore of the Churchill River and called it Fort Prince of Wales. For food, the Europeans had to rely on the Cree and the Dene, who were at war with each other. Although the Europeans had in the late seventeenth century been able to attract the Cree to York Factory by offering various incentives, the Dene weren't eager to abandon the caribou hunt for the sake of the fur trade.[6]

In his journals, James Knight, who was the Governor of the HBC in 1717, described the first breakthrough towards peace between the Cree and the Dene, and the initiation of the Dene into the fur trade. Knight said it was a Dene woman named Thanadelthur — a slave captured by the Cree and who had come to the HBC trading post in 1713 with her Cree captors — who arranged the first meeting between her people and HBC traders. Among all the Dene peoples, the Sayisi Dene became the first to be drawn into the fur trade.[7]

The records of the HBC show that, by the middle of the eighteenth century, the "Chipewyans" were playing a role requiring great intelligence and skill, acting as middlemen between the Company and the other Dene tribes in more remote areas. But they continued to suffer from escalating wars with the Cree and from the diseases they caught from the Europeans. During the eighteenth century, the population of Dene peoples throughout the Canadian Northwest was substantially reduced by epidemics of chicken pox, scarlet fever, smallpox, cholera, influenza, and whooping cough.[8] Samuel Hearne believed that nine-tenths of the Northern Indians had died from diseases introduced by the Europeans.[9]

Throughout the rest of the eighteenth century, competition in the northern fur trade grew as the HBC and the North West Company fought for dominance. But the Sayisi Dene were interested in hunting caribou more for their own needs than for the fur trade. In 1767, Hearne wrote that the caribou provided so much of the Chipewyan's needs that only a few furs were needed to provide them with the new necessities of life.[10] In contrast, the survival of the Europeans depended on the Sayisi Dene. Trading-post managers who couldn't hunt or bring in food from the south persuaded a group of Sayisi Dene hunters to stay near the post and look after the "whites." The hunters who agreed to stay near the trading post in Churchill came to be called Homeguard Chipewyans.[11]

Meanwhile, the majority of the Sayisi Dene continued to follow caribou herds, as they had done for many centuries, occasionally trading meat and furs for things like guns and ammunition. They would come to Churchill once a year, in spring, to trade.

In the nineteenth century, the European influence in the North greatly increased with the arrival of European and Canadian missionaries who began to convert Aboriginal peoples to Christianity. Many missionaries learned Aboriginal languages and translated Christian hymns and prayers into Dene. HBC records show that the first baptism for Fort Churchill Chipewyan took place in 1865. By the end of the century, Christian rituals and practices were widely performed in the Northwest, while deeply rooted traditional spiritual beliefs also lived on.[12]

BETSY ANDERSON

I remember a time when there were no white men (*bonlai*)[13] around us, and the people had to survive on the land. This was a very long time ago. The people were instinctive and strong like the caribou and the wolves in this harsh territory. Their sense of direction when they travelled was unfailing as if the directions were imprinted in their minds. They didn't need a map. They just knew where to go. The people were in tune with the land and with the animals on the land.

Our people were constantly on the move. We travelled from one location to another, on foot. Clans of families usually walked together. We spent the winters in the shelter of trees, but in the summer we usually moved north and camped beside a large lake or river. I remember many summers near the Churchill River because at the time of spring break-up many of our men went there to trade.

Survival was hard work. To eat, we had to hunt or fish. To stay warm, we had to make caribou-hide clothes. For shelter, we had to make our own teepees. There were no short cuts. We did everything by hand. We went everywhere on foot. Never once did anyone complain about the hard work. No one ever got angry because there was so much work to do. We had to co-operate, there was no time to argue. It was just the way our life was.

The men hunted. The women did all the other work. Our people believed women are stronger than men, so women carried all the loads. Women got the wood, prepared the food, sewed all the clothes, and looked after the children. We hauled water from a hole cut through ice as thick as a person's height.

If our clan made a decision to make a move the next day, the men would go to hunt for the journey. The women would pack up everything. They would take down the camp, pack whatever they could on sleds, and they would pull this load of household goods and clothes along with their small children. Some of the women would be driving dog-teams with heavy loads.

Everyone had clothes made of caribou hide with the fur on it. It's surprising when I think about it now, how light and warm those clothes were. Our blankets, pillows and mattresses were also made of caribou skins with the hair still on them. Caribou blankets were usually shaped like a sleeping bag, made out of three hides. The women wore caribou-hair jackets sewn together with white fur trim and with fringes at the bottom. All the women, young and old, wore the same style of dress and coats with a wide belt tied in the middle.

On the day of the move, everyone in the camp would get up before sunrise, while it was still dark. The men would eat a meal of dried caribou meat with fat, and they would set out to break trail for us women and children who would be following behind.

All the children old enough to walk had snowshoes. Children's snowshoes were made with a string of caribou hide to tie over their feet so the shoes wouldn't fall off when they were walking. In those days, if a child was able to walk, she had to walk. We didn't think for a minute that we should carry little children. All people young and old had to pull loads of household things and clothing on a sled. Even the children were pulling small sleds. Some of the young mothers would have special sleds lined with caribou fur for their babies.

The men always walked ahead of the women, looking for any sign of caribou herds. In winter, they would be wearing hand-made snowshoes made of caribou hides and pulling a sled behind them. When they reached an area with trees for shelter that would be good for an overnight camp, they would prepare a place for us by cutting and piling up firewood. They would leave their loads there at the campsite, and go to hunt caribou.

If they found caribou, they would bring some carcasses back to the campsite so that when the women and the children reached the campsite there would be food there. When we, the women and children, reached that spot, we would unload our gear for our overnight camp. We would pitch up the tents and cook a meal with whatever we had. If the men had shot caribou, the women would prepare and preserve the meat so we could use it for a long time. I remember the excitement of everyone in the group as we prepared to settle down for the night.

As soon as evening fell we would go to sleep. It wasn't hard after a long day of walking. Even when the weather was cold it didn't bother us at all, it just seemed so pleasant to prepare a new place to sleep. The elders would say to us, "Look out for the first sight of dawn on the horizon." They wanted to move as soon as possible. Time was valuable because there was so much to do in a day, and such long distances to travel. They were always in such a rush all the time, and now not one of those people is alive. Only myself.

In winter, men went trapping for furs. They walked all over the bush even when there were no roads or paths. The winter weather was bitterly cold, but it didn't bother them. It was the only way to live. It was our way for survival from the beginning of time.

This is how our people walked from one area to another looking for good hunting and trapping grounds. This is how I travelled with my people all over the land. There were times when our people struggled to survive. We suffered from shortages of food, but we never looked upon ourselves as helpless. We never felt doomed.

When there were lots of caribou, women made tents in the shape of a teepee out of caribou hides. When I was a young child, I saw older women working all day long to tan the hides. They would scrape the flesh away from the inside of the hides, they would soak the hides in water and cut off the hair. Then, they would put the hides away until the weather turned cold. In late fall, they would boil mashed caribou brain mixed with water in a large tub and they would soak the caribou hides in that boiled brain to bleach and soften the hides. They would hang the hides outside where they would freeze, and where the wind would dry them. You would see rows and rows of white caribou hides hanging high on poles at the camp. It was a beautiful sight.

The women would talk excitedly about the tasks that still lay ahead of them. When they took the hides back inside, they tied them in bundles, one hide at a time, and hung them up near the smoke hole of the teepee so the hide would turn yellow from the smoke. The next step was to soak the hide once more in luke-warm water with caribou brain in it, to wring it out and to hang it to dry, like a piece of cloth. After that, the hide was smoked once more. They had to use the right kind of moss and willow branches for the smoke, or the hide could be ruined. During the night I used to see older women sitting there and softening the hides by scraping them with tools made out of caribou or moose bone. Preparing the hides was the responsibility of older women, but the task of sewing the teepee belonged to young women.

When all the hides were tanned and ready to be cut and sewn together to make the big teepee, the older women would prepare a place by picking a spot and laying spruce branches over a large area on the ground. They would lay the skins down and cut the hides. They would then call out and tell all the young women that it was time to start sewing.

The young women would come together to unravel the sinew they used as thread and make it into strands. This took time. By the time they were finished doing this, there would be piles of sinew on the ground. The weather was already cold, so the people would make a big campfire, and the sewing would start. If your hands got cold you could warm them up at the fire, but you had to keep sewing. They used to say it took thirty hides to make one teepee, so it was a very large tent, and heavy.

They would cut out a little shape like a glove for the tip of the teepee. The teepee poles would fit into that shape. There would be a big pole at the centre. When the young women finished sewing one side of the tent, they would turn it over and start on the other side. They sewed strands of hide to tie the tent into place at the top, on the sides and at the entrance. It was a lot of hard work, but it was worth it.

I remember how happy I felt once the teepee was put up, and they put moss all around it, and we were ready to move in it. It was so clean and so bright that it felt like a whole new world. The sun shone on it during the day, and in the evening, from the outside, you could see the lights glowing inside.

There would be two or three families living in one teepee. It was large and wide. We all helped each other and gathered and hauled wood until there were piles and piles by the tents. This wood didn't last long once the weather got cold, especially if the women were tanning caribou hides. The good feeling of being in a new teepee would last until the tent became dirty from the smoke. By then, it would be time to move somewhere else.

In the old days we weren't supposed to tell stories about the Cree. Maybe our people were superstitious and too scared of being attacked.

The Cree were the first to have any contact with the white man. During those days, the Cree would kill the Sayisi Dene whenever they had a chance. They were already trading with the Europeans and they had access to rifles and ammunition. With this new weapon, they had the upper hand on the Sayisi Dene, and they started to wipe out our people.

There's an old story about the Sayisi Dene's first contact with the white man. I heard it from my elders, when I was a young woman. They said the Cree had taken two Sayisi Dene slaves named Bekkenshies and Kaiyuseh. The Cree were travelling with these two slaves, using them to haul heavy loads, to hunt and to keep camp, treating the slaves like dogs.

When they reached Fort Prince of Wales to trade their pelts with the white man, they told the two Dene slaves to wait at the campsite. They said the people the white men were going to see would kill the Dene if they saw them. But when the Cree traders set out for the fort, the slaves decided to sneak up behind them to see who they were meeting. The slave named Bekkenshies followed the Cree. As the Cree approached the gate, they realized that one of the slaves was behind them.

But they couldn't do anything because the people inside the fort had already opened the gate to let them in. The gate was a large stone that was rolled back to open the door into the fort. As they went in, Bekkenshies crept in behind them. The story goes that the slave figured, "The Cree have killed all my people already. If they want to kill me too, I'm ready to die."

Once they were inside, the Englishman who was the head of the fort kept looking only at the Dene slave and not at the Cree. The Cree started to walk back and forth in front of the slave in order to cut off the view of the Englishman. But the Englishman still continued to look towards the slave. His stare made the slave think what the Cree told him had been true, that he was going to be killed.

Then the Englishman spoke: "Is he one of your people?" The Cree said, "Yes, he is." Then Bekkenshies said, "I am not one of their people. I am a Sayisi Dene slave. They have killed many of my people. I haul their sleds for them. Usually they tell me to stay back at the campsite until they return from this fort, but I wanted to see for myself what kind of people they were trading with, so I followed them here. They told me you would kill me."

The Englishman turned to the Cree. "You told us that you were using the guns we give you to kill people who were no better than animals. But it appears that you were killing people that are just as good as you, if not better. This fort was put here because we know of a race of people who use this territory and we need their help and their skills to help us explore this land. We could use the furs they will trade with us." Then the Englishman asked Bekkenshies if he was the only slave. "No," said Bekkenshies. "There is one more back at the camp in the bush." The Englishman then told the Cree to go and bring the other slave back to the fort, alive.

The two slaves were taken to the living quarters of the English, and they were bathed and given clean clothes. When they came out, the Englishman said, "These people do not look like animals, they are handsome." The slaves were asked again if others like them were alive in the Cree territory. They said, "Yes, there are also two women slaves." The English then sent for the Dene women. They were also brought back to the fort.

The winter passed and the spring came and the Dene slaves stayed at the fort. The head of the fort kept asking them if any of their people were alive. The slaves didn't know. They told the English that until the Cree were given guns, they, the Dene, had always managed to defend themselves. But once the Cree started using guns, they could wipe out the Sayisi Dene.

The English decided to set out on foot to look for Sayisi Dene survivors. They loaded supplies on sleds, they took the Dene slaves with them and went towards the north. They reached a place called South Henik Lake. In those days, that area was our traditional territory. Our people hunted caribou on the barren lands to the north of South Henik Lake. To make a fire to cook, they had to use a moss that grew there because there are no trees on that land, and no bush. There, they found some Sayisi Dene people. That's when the first contact was made between the Sayisi Dene and the white people.

Kaiyuseh led the Englishmen to a big hill at South Henik Lake. He told them that if any Dene were alive and camping in the region, they would flee upon seeing the strangers because they would take them for the Cree. He said he would climb to the top of the hill, alone.

On top of the hill, Kaiyuseh crept along a big rock, and as he looked down, he could see people at a camp. He could see a group of people playing a game chasing a ball. He could hear laughter. He felt great relief that some of his people had survived.

But the people in the camp had noticed someone was spying on them from behind a rock. They always counted each and every rock — and watched out for anything unusual in the landscape. At the first suspicious sight, they would gather up their things and flee. So Kaiyuseh quickly made a fire with the moss.

The elders in the camp said, "Why would the Cree make a fire? It looks like it's someone who wants to talk to us." They asked the younger men to check who it was. Kaiyuseh then called out. "Do not be scared," he said. "Do not run away. I am Kaiyuseh who you thought was killed by the Cree long ago. I'm with a group of people who won't kill you. Don't run." This message was relayed back to the camp, and then the people came to meet Kaiyuseh.

They had never seen people with white skin before. The people who saw the white men described them like this: "Long pieces of metal stuck out of their mouths, and fire was escaping out of them." They meant that the white men were smoking pipes with tobacco. Kaiyuseh said, "The southern Indians making all that noise and smoke were getting their noisemakers from people who come from far away." He then signalled to the white men, so they came into view.

The Dene were in shock and in awe of what they came face to face with. The white men looked as if they were carrying caribou hindquarters over their shoulders. (They were carrying guns and ammunition belts that criss-crossed over their shoulders and chests.) Their brimmed hats were like giant mushrooms. Fire and smoke were bouncing off their bodies and trailing behind them. Their eyes were like seagulls' eyes, looking at the people.

The Englishmen gave all the people a drag of their tobacco. It affected some of them — especially the ones who were medicine men. Then the white men gave our people supplies: knives, axes, and files. The white men then told our people that if they traded pelts at the fort, they would get supplies like these and other materials, and food, in return. That winter, the Sayisi Dene took some caribou hides and beaver pelts to the fort for trading. The former slave, Bekkenshies, was appointed to an important position in the fort. The people looked up to him as a boss. That's how it began.

In spring, people travelled to the trading post in Churchill, and stayed there for a short while. Sometimes we stayed in one place through the summer. It was the longest time when we weren't moving. As winter approached, the sleds had to be made and all the clothes had to be prepared and then we would be on the move again to another location.

I remember a time when I was a young girl and we were walking from the big trading post in Churchill to Nejanilini Lake where my grandfather had spent the summer. I think we were going to pick him up and go south to our hunting grounds. I was with my mother, my father, and my three brothers. I was just a young child, but I was strong enough to walk.

It was late fall, the weather was cold, and I was hungry. It was one of those years when there was no sign of caribou anywhere. The only way to get food was to set a net in fishing holes along the way. If the fishing was good we stayed for a couple of days. (Some people would fish with a stick and bait tied at the end of a long strand of hide.) When we caught fish, we had a meal for the day. Then we would travel again. Between the fishing holes, there was usually nothing to eat, except the berries on the ground. We would stop and collect the berries. That could be a daily meal too. Just berries.

When we came to a river we had to cross, the people would chop trees down and throw them in the water. They would chop spruce branches and make a sort of bridge for the crossing. In summer there was a lot of water everywhere because the ground was permanently frozen and it didn't absorb anything. In fall, that water would start to freeze up, and you could see all the black spots on the water where people had crossed the rivers by using branches. Those branches froze into the ground or on the rivers and left dark spots in the ice.

I remember on that one trip when we were hungry all the time, two men came to our campsite one evening. It had started snowing. The two Sayisi Dene men who showed up were wet and cold. They told my father they had not seen any caribou all summer. They said they were also short of food, and that, like us, they were living on fish alone.

The next day, wet snow was falling. We didn't have any rubber footwear in those days, just our wrap-around moccasins. My father decided to leave with those two men, to look for caribou or beaver. My little brother Moses went with my father. I was left with my mother, and my brother David and my baby brother. My mother was carrying my baby brother on her back in a cradle-board. We set out on our own. In those days, our people were never afraid to walk alone. There was no fear of any kind. You were just connected to the land around you.

We walked all that day and made camp for the night. It was very cold and snowing. My mother had a small .22-calibre rifle. She went to hunt ptarmigans with it. She managed to shoot one. Four of us shared this small bird. This was our only meal for the next few days, but we still kept walking. We came to a small river and crossed it. Then, my mother made a fire to make some tea. As we were sitting beside the campfire near the shoreline, I noticed a ripple above the water and I said to my mother, "Look over there!" My mother took her gun and went to check it out. It was a fish! My mother shot into the water, hit it, caught it as it was floating away, and she brought it back to us. She cooked it over the campfire. That was our second meal in three days.

The next day, we kept walking, and we came to a bigger river. It was still snowing. We crossed the river by walking into the water. My mother was carrying my little brothers. After we crossed, we came to a place where there were some trees, and we had shelter from the wind. My mother shot some small birds, whisky-jacks. I boiled them for my little brother David, but my mother and I didn't have anything to eat.

A little later, my mother took off her load and the baby cradle and set them on the ground so we could have a short rest. She told me and my little brother to collect some blackberries. As we were looking for patches of blackberries under the snow, we saw two women walking towards us. The word had got back to the camp ahead of us that we were on our way and without food. These women were bringing us fish. People shared everything in those days. It was the only way to survive. Anyway, my mother fed us. While we ate, she visited with her women friends. Then we started walking again. We walked miles and miles like that.

After another long day of walking, we heard the voice of my aunt Sophie in the bush behind us. We waited to see if it really was her. As it turned out, she had been looking for us all over the land. She had gone on a different trail. When it got dark she had found a sheltered place, she had cleared it and crawled in and gone to sleep for the night. We all laughed and prepared a meal with the fish she had brought us.

Life was hard during those times when the caribou was scarce. Sometimes the weather would suddenly change and a north wind would rise. It would be blowing and snowing for days and days. The men couldn't put the birch-bark canoes into the lake to take the fish nets out of the water, the waves would be too high. As it got colder, the rivers started to freeze over and all the fish nets froze. This created more hardships for the people because we depended on the nets to get fish. Some people had fishing poles with bait on the end of a long string. Some days there would be nothing to eat at all. Our people also made traps to catch martens. They would freeze two pieces of peeled twigs or branches from a small willow bush, and hang them up in the shape of an X. Sometimes birds would land on those twigs and get caught. I used to go with my father when he was trapping for martens. Once I trapped a lot of martens in my trap made of sticks. I remember this because I was very pleased. I went to the trading post and bought some beads for myself.

The people lived like this until a herd of caribou came. When hunters saw caribou tracks, they knew the herd was near. But it was a long time before the first caribou would be shot.

Before the port or the railway or the town were built, Churchill had a trading post, a post manager, a minister, and a few Métis people. No one else. When our people travelled there in spring, we all stayed in white canvas tents. Our people would set up rows of identical tents that looked neat and attractive on the shores of the Churchill River.

The people would set fish nets in the bay or up the river. Someone would go to check the nets for the catch and bring back a boat full of fish to our camp. We would all go to the boat with small pails or bags and everyone would get a share of the catch.

I remember how we would all look towards Hudson Bay to see who would be the first to sight the steamboat. In those days the big boats would run on coal, and there would be thick black smoke rising from the chimney. While we waited for this ship to arrive, we lived on fish only. There was nothing else. There would be nothing at the trading post except tea. Sometimes there was cornmeal, yellow and lumpy. We used to call it dog meal. But if there was nothing else, we would make bannock out of it. It wasn't as good as real flour but you got a meal out of it.

At times there was no fish either. We used to set nets in the middle of the night without any light. The elders told us young people not to make a fire because the light would attract bears. If we made a fire it had to be so small that its reflection wouldn't shine on the water. People would never do that today. There was one woman who had a homemade lantern with a candle in it. She would sometimes bring this lantern with her, and we would follow behind her. It seemed like such a bright light. We checked the nets when the tide was out.

After checking the nets and setting them again, we would set out in the early hours of the morning and reach home at the first sight of dawn. We would sleep for a little while, then get up, do our chores, and wait for the tide to go out. Then we would go and check our fish nets again. The people did this day after day. It was the only way to eat. We didn't have rubber boots, we just had wrap-around moccasins. When I think back, I realize I must have been a very strong young woman to have lived in those days and to still be here today to talk about it.

Some people went way up the shoreline of Hudson Bay to hunt small ducks. After a couple of days, they would return with bags of ducks to feed the family. We lived like this all summer until the steamship came in with supplies.

When the ship finally came in, all the men would go across to where it would be unloaded. They would help to unload the supplies into this huge warehouse, which had four doors. The Cree and the Inuit would also come into Churchill around that time to help with the unloading. There was a crane that belonged to the steamship. It was used to haul crates on boats below. Then the boats would go to the shore where the warehouse was. The boats would go back and forth until all the supplies were hauled from the ship into the warehouse. Some of the supplies would go up north into the Eskimo country, and some would go towards the Cree country in the south, towards York Factory, and some of the supplies stayed in Churchill.

The people who worked as labourers to unload the ship would be paid the equivalent of three beaver pelts for one day's work. It was approximately one dollar and fifty cents. A woman whose husband was helping unload this ship could walk into the trading post and receive food supplies from the trading-post manager. If the women and children had already taken supplies from the trading post on credit, the men would get nothing because their earnings would barely pay off the debt.

The Dene stayed near Churchill through the summer. In fall we would move back to our hunting grounds.

I remember one of the days when we left Churchill to begin our long walk back to the forest. A wet snow was falling, a cold wind was blowing, and the ice was forming around the shoreline of Hudson Bay. All the women were hauling loads on their backs, some were carrying babies in a cradle on their backs, and this didn't prevent them from carrying other loads. The dogs were also loaded with packs tied to their backs. Small children were walking. I remember that particular trip because it was a very rough one. In my lifetime I have been through many hard times, but this was one of the worst.

We were walking along the Hudson Bay shoreline up the coast towards the north. We had to cross many small rivers along the way. It was bitterly cold, and the river crossings were deep. The load I was carrying was heavy. A wide belt made out of caribou hide ran across my forehead — this was to support the heavy load that was attached to this head belt — this is how we, the women, carried heavy loads. I guess it's easier to carry heavy packs that way.

When we came to a river, we had to walk across it, you had no other choice. But before we crossed the river, we would put our loads down — people would pass them to each other — like a relay — to get them to the other shore. They did the same thing with small children — pass them from person to person. Once we got to the other side of the river safely, we would pack our things on our backs, support them with that head belt, and continue to walk. We would reach another river crossing and do the same thing over and over again. It was the only way.

We kept crossing those streams. The water would reach up to my chest at times. The weather was cold and the water was colder. I remember my father had brought a canvas tent and a stove with stove pipes. It was our most valuable possession, and my mother was carrying it on her back.

After walking all day and crossing rivers and streams, we would select a spot to camp for the night. My family had a new tent so we slept well. But some families had nothing. We all helped one another. There was not a dry spot of ground any-where. There was water all around. We would pile up willows and spruce bars until the water was covered. Then we would pitch our teepee on that surface.

The next morning we started to walk again. It was snowing, with a high wind from the north. We kept walking. After a while I had no feeling in my feet at all, as if I got used to walking in the ice-cold water with only moccasins on my feet.

After we reached barren land, the weather changed and the sun came out, and the wind was warmer. We travelled the rest of the way in this nice weather.

The Sayisi Dene are one tough people. I must have been a strong young woman. During those years, the people were as fierce as the cold winters and the vast land which stretched as far as the eye could see.

My mother taught me how to deliver babies. She told me I should know how to do it because you never know when you may be near a woman whose time has come and there may be no one else around. So I went with my mother when she was helping women give birth. I learned by watching, and I became a midwife. I deliv-ered many babies, some of whom are still alive today.

When a woman was ready to deliver her baby, she would send for any women nearby who could help. Even if they were travelling from camp to camp, the women would call out to each other when their time came. There was nothing hard about it. They would prepare a shelter — even outdoors in winter. They would make a fire with spruce boughs and dry branches, melt some snow, and boil water. When the baby's head started to show, they would put a clean cloth against its mouth as it was coming out of the womb. They would gently ease the baby out.

When the baby was out, any one of the women present could come forward to cut the cord and tie it securely with a caribou sinew. They would clean the baby's mouth, and an elder would breathe into the baby's mouth to give it air.

But when I delivered babies, I delivered them inside — either in a tent or in a cabin, not outdoors. I would ask for a container of luke-warm water and as soon as the baby came out, instead of breathing into his mouth, I would immediately bathe it. As soon as I put the baby in that water, it would start to cry.

We would treat the placenta very carefully, and bury it in the ground in some moss. We used a kind of lichen moss that grows in the tundra to absorb the blood flowing from the mother. We wrapped her in caribou skins and soon she would be strong enough to continue the journey.

TREATY FIVE

In 1870, the Dominion of Canada took control of the northwestern territory of British North America from the HBC.[1] Soon afterwards, the government began to open up the prairies for settlement. In southern Manitoba, the land was suitable for agriculture and for commerce. Between 1871 and 1876, Canada signed five different treaties with the Aboriginal peoples who lived in southern Manitoba. With the treaties, the Aboriginal peoples "transferred, surrendered and relinquished to His Majesty the King . . . all rights, title and privilege . . . in the territory described,"[2] in return for reserve land.

But government officials considered the land north of the Manitoba Interlake, extending into the sub-arctic, too harsh for settlement. They didn't believe it could be of much economic value to the people of Canada. Despite repeated requests from northern Aboriginal leaders, the government did not begin the process of signing treaties with northern Aboriginal peoples for another thirty years.

During the first decade of the twentieth century, the federal government became convinced of the economic potential of northern Manitoba. Plans were already in the works to extend further north to Churchill the railroad that went from Winnipeg to The Pas. The northern extension of the railway would cut through "unceded" land occupied by Aboriginal peoples. The easiest way to clear title for the railway was to sign treaties with the northern peoples.

But instead of negotiating a new treaty, the government offered northern Aboriginal peoples "adhesions" to Treaty Five. It was the cheapest option. Treaty Ten, which had been signed with other Aboriginal peoples in Saskatchewan and Manitoba in 1906, would have provided Aboriginal peoples with a much larger land base than Treaty Five (Treaty Ten would give 640 acres to each family rather than the 160 acres to each family under Treaty Five). The process of negotiation and signing of these adhesions to Treaty Five seems to have been, according to historian Frank Tough, "a transparent case of a one-sided use of authority" carried out "solely at the convenience of the government."[3]

The Sayisi Dene were almost the last of the northern Aboriginal peoples to sign an adhesion to Treaty Five. On August 1, 1910, they gathered at Fort Prince of Wales (north of Churchill) to negotiate. A former Methodist missionary, Reverend John Semmens, was the commissioner responsible for negotiating the treaty with the Northern Indians. Semmens led the small government group. A journalist with the *Toronto Star Weekly* accompanied Semmens and left this record of his view of the "negotiations" between the Dominion of Canada and the Sayisi Dene: "When the Commissioner had finished [a brief speech], . . . some of the leading Chipewyans expressed concern for their hunting rights. If they give up their land to the Government, would they have the right to hunt as their fathers had done before them? If they were not allowed to hunt, they would starve. They had heard about a railway being built to bring the white man to Churchill; how would that affect them? Would they have to live within the reserve which the Government would give them?" The journalist, A.V. Thomas, also reported that Semmens had assured the Sayisi Dene that "not for many years to come, probably not in the lifetime of any of them, would their hunting right be interfered with."[4]

The whole process of negotiation seems to have lasted no more than a few hours. The treaty contained words and concepts for which the Dene language had no equivalent — words such as *rights, title, privilege, acre, longitude,* and *latitude.* Even with an interpreter, the two sides couldn't communicate clearly. Thomas reported that "the communications [Semmens] received from the band through an interpreter were unsatisfactory and nebulous."[5] The treaty was signed with three X's.

The Sayisi Dene were now called the Fort Churchill Chipewyan Band. After that summer day in 1910, they celebrated Treaty Day each year with a drum dance. The Dominion of Canada had laid claim to the natural resources of the Sayisi Dene homeland in return for five dollars per adult per year, and an annual visit by a doctor. Soon, the RCMP and the Indian agent became new actors on the northern scene.

BETSY ANDERSON

I am now the only one still alive to talk about that time in our history. All the others are dead.

At that time, our people lived scattered over a vast land and travelled all over our traditional territory. They didn't stay in one place all together. That made it hard for them to meet in one place. My elders told me the treaty was supposed to have been signed in 1909, but that year many of the Sayisi Dene didn't make it near Churchill. So it was in 1910 that the signing of the treaty between the Sayisi Dene and the Crown of England took place.

That day is as clear in my mind as if it were today. All the Sayisi Dene gathered near Churchill, at a spot north of Fort Prince of Wales. A big steamship came from York Factory, bringing the RCMP and other white men who would be at the signing of the treaty. All the people were told that the treaty would take place that day. We saw the ship coming in, and the people coming off, and we all went down to where the meeting place was set up. It was the first time I'd seen the RCMP. We were told they were to be feared. All of us kids sat down and didn't dare to move as we watched them walk around in their bright red suits. All the Sayisi Dene men were called to the place where the ceremony would take place.

The white men told the Dene that all other Native groups had signed treaties, and that we were just one of those groups. I remember that the treaty was signed without proper translation. The Dene didn't fully understand what was in it. We just assumed it was a peace treaty and that from then on, the white men would help us by providing us more supplies like flour and guns.

The land was not talked about. The way we understood that piece of paper, the land was not part of the deal. If we had been told that we were signing away our land for the amount of five dollars a person, there was no way our people would have agreed. There were many good people who lived in those days. Our elders were intelligent. They would never have agreed to such a crazy idea. If we had understood the white man's language, there would have been a very tough negotiation with the Dene. But we didn't understand it. The Dene thought the white man was giving us money to help us out because we needed more of their equipment.

Our people were not asked who we would choose as our chief and councillors. Perhaps the men talked among themselves and decided who would talk best for the people. Until then we did not know what a chief and council were. That is something designed by the white man. We used to have our leaders in our clans — they would be the best hunters or the ones who were the most skilled in leading the people and giving them directions on survival. But on that day, three leaders were chosen to sign the treaty. The name of the man chosen chief was John French. He held that title until he died. Those newly chosen leaders were not paid for holding their titles, but on Treaty Days the chief would be paid an additional ten dollars, and the councillors were paid five dollars on top of their treaty money.

So, on that August day in 1910, the new chief came out and told the people he would call each family by name, and the man whose name was called out would come with his wife and his children, get registered and be given treaty money of five dollars each. It seemed like millions of dollars were being given to us. It took two days for all the people to be registered. There were a lot of people in those days. (Now only 400 Sayisi Dene are left alive; it would only take an hour or two to record all our names. So many of our people have died).

At the end of the two days, the new chief, John French, was asked to sit down on a chair set up for him. The white people draped a Canadian flag over him. They told the Sayisi Dene, "This is your new leader, your chief." I was sitting with my mother and a group of other women and children.

Shortly after this, the RCMP came out and they hauled bags of food supplies and piled them in a corner. A share of this food came with the treaty payout. The basic supply consisted of salt pork, flour, lard, sugar, tea, tobacco, and ammunition. After that day, every year on Treaty Day, we would be given a food supply and some ammunition.

When the treaty registration was over, the white man said to the Dene: "From this day on, you will never be in need of food supplies. This will always be provided for you. Have a feast and then you will celebrate this day. It's an event which is celebrated all over this country." The people then spread a wide white canvas on the ground and they started preparing the food for the feast. They cooked bannock, made two huge pails of tea and poured milk into the tea. They also roasted some meat. Then the people gathered to eat together.

When the feast was over and everything was cleaned up, it was time for the most important thing. For me as a child, this was the highlight of the whole event. They filled this big wide bowl with candy and passed it around to us. When it came to me, I was excited and I thought, It's really true that only good things will happen for us from now on. The white men will provide only good things for us from this day on. The candy tasted so sweet, it was the best thing I had ever tasted. Our lives, our future from now on will be like this candy, I was thinking, Sweet and good.

As they prepared a place for a fiddle dance, they sent the children back to the campsite with some of the old grannies. The grannies put us to bed. Children were never allowed to go out after dark. We were very disciplined. We respected our parents and elders.

Today, eighty-five years later, I live in a little matchbox house with no running water or proper heat. Of my eleven children, nine have died alcohol-related deaths during our days of poverty in Churchill. I often wish I had pictures of my children who died, so I could look back and remember what they looked like. But I don't.

The white men haven't kept their promises. They have all the power now because they have our land. But as the only person alive who remembers that historic day in 1910, I have something the white men don't have: my memory, which is as clear as it was when I was a child. I am richer than they are in that sense. I am a wealthy woman.

DUCK LAKE

The signing of Treaty Five had little immediate effect on the lives of the Sayisi Dene. After 1910, they began to gather once a year at Fort Prince of Wales near Churchill to receive their treaty money, some food provisions, and to celebrate Treaty Days with drum songs and dances. The Fort Churchill Chipewyan Band had no reserve. Nor did it have a political organization that could deal adequately with the Canadian government. Most of the year, the people lived in small groups scattered over the land. The only function of the chief and council was to be present during the annual Treaty Days. There were no group issues to deal with, no funds to administer, no programs to carry out.

But the Canadian North was changing. A year after the Sayisi Dene signed Treaty Five, the Government of Canada established the present border between Manitoba and the Northwest Territories. The Sayisi Dene were hardly aware of this administrative detail, but it meant that a political line now divided their traditional lands. During the next four decades, more events in the "white man's world," events unknown to and out of the control of the Dene, eventually closed in on them.

Early in the new century, steamboats and railways opened up the North to many new seekers of fortune, including aggressive and ambitious non-Aboriginal trappers. Unlike the Dene or the Cree, who never over-trapped and who stayed away from each other's trap lines, the non-Aboriginal trappers were eager to harvest as many pelts as possible within as short a time as possible. They brought steel traps and poisoned bait. They did not hesitate to trespass on Dene hunting grounds and trap lines. One Indian agent reported, "[These trappers are] so ruthless in their trapping methods, that whenever they trap they kill off every thing completely if possible and leave nothing for future years."[1] Philip Godsell, who was a trader in northern Manitoba in the 1920s, later wrote that in one season the new "professional trapper" would "accumulate three or four times as much as an entire Indian family has been in the habit of taking out of the same territory over a period of years."[2] The Dene resented this intrusion, and they hated the poisoned bait because it killed their dogs. Soon, they also noticed there were fewer animals on their lands.

The Government of Canada noticed it too. Various groups in the North had begun to lobby Ottawa. The HBC was asking the government to regulate the fur trade to reduce the plunder of fur-bearing animals by free traders, the Dene wanted the government to defend their rights against the intruders, and missionaries wanted the government to protect "natives" from the alcohol, prostitution, and violence that they associated with the newcomers.[3] Government officials came to a simple conclusion: heavy demands on wildlife were threatening important species like beaver, caribou, and wood bison. In 1917, in response to these lobby efforts, Parliament passed the North West Game Act, prohibiting the hunting of certain animals (like wood bison) and setting specific seasons for others. This was the beginning of a new approach to northern wildlife management.[4] It was a far cry from what the Aboriginal people wanted, however; in fact, it was harmful to the Dene peoples across the Canadian Northwest, including the Sayisi Dene.

The Canadian government had also decided to use Churchill as a gateway to the Arctic. In 1928, the railway from the south finally reached the shores of Hudson Bay. The government built a port and a grain elevator in Churchill, and surveyed the area for a townsite. From then on, the population of Churchill fluctuated greatly between summer and winter. During summer months, up to 3,500 men lived and worked there,[5] and in winter, that number dropped to fifty or less. The permanent residents were mainly the employees of the HBC, or were Anglican missionaries or RCMP. The development of a community at Churchill dealt a blow to the HBC's monopoly on the fur trade, because the way to the sub-arctic frontier was now open to many competitors. By the time the Depression began to affect fur prices, the Company had begun to close some of its trading posts and to reduce its personnel in the North.

In 1930, the Dominion Government turned control of crown lands and natural resources over to the provincial governments of Manitoba, Alberta, and Saskatchewan — all of whom were serious about regulating the fur trade. Now a *second* distant government — the provincial government — would also have an influence on the lives of the Sayisi Dene. A clause in the Natural Resources Transfer Agreement stated that the Government of Canada agreed to recognize provincial game laws as applying to Aboriginal peoples, provided that they continued to have the right to hunt, trap, and fish on unoccupied crown land or on other lands to which they might have a "right of access."[6] During the thirties, the provincial governments began to implement a complex system of game regulations that included closed seasons on beaver, muskrat, marten, moose, and caribou.

Now, provincial game wardens across the Canadian Northwest began to pressure Dene hunters and trappers to respect seasonal restrictions. This was confusing and upsetting for people who believed that the treaties guaranteed their hunting and fishing rights. Throughout the North, Aboriginal peoples objected to these hunting restrictions on the grounds that they violated guarantees they had been given during treaty negotiations. No one listened to them.[7]

Duck Lake and North River

While social and political forces were changing southern Canadians' attitudes about the North, the Sayisi Dene continued their traditional way of life. The treaty that they had signed at Fort Prince of Wales allotted each family of five an area of 160 acres. There had been some talk of a "permanent" settlement. The Sayisi Dene told the government they wanted to stay inland, near their traditional hunting grounds. In 1914, Indian Affairs had attempted a survey to set up a reserve for them, but the process was never completed. In the mid-twenties, Indian Affairs considered settling the Sayisi Dene at Reindeer Lake, close to the Dene community of Lac Brochet in northwestern Manitoba, but the Anglican bishop opposed the move because he thought he might lose the Anglicans to the Catholic mission at Lac Brochet.[8] The Fort Churchill Chipewyan Band remained without a reserve. Its members continued to spend the year living throughout the interior of northern Manitoba and the Northwest Territories until the end of the twenties. Many of them visited Churchill for a short time each year in summer.

They did have favourite campsites. The shores of some of the lakes on the edge of the barren grounds sustained them year after year. Caribou Lake, about 100 kilometres northwest of Churchill, was one of them. Another 100 kilometres to the northwest, in the heart of the Sayisi Dene's traditional territory, lay interconnected lakes dotted with islands — Nejanilini Lake, Duck Lake, and Little Duck Lake — all surrounded by patches of forest and barren grounds with long esker ridges. Fish were abundant in the large lakes, and ducks and geese were plentiful.

But more important, the narrows to the north of Duck Lake were on a major caribou migration path. Each fall, the Beverly Kaminuriak herd would turn south from the barren grounds and cross the lake on its way to the transition forest.[9] The Sayisi Dene had big fall hunts at Duck Lake before they, too, migrated south and west to the shelter of trees for winter. The fall hunt provided them and their dogs with food through the winter.

In 1930, the HBC moved its trading post, which had been in Churchill for 250 years, about 120 kilometres northwest, to Caribou Lake, and called it Caribou Post. The new post was closer to the Sayisi Dene trappers, and the HBC hoped to prevent free traders from offering better prices to the Dene. However, there was not enough firewood at Caribou Lake to sustain a community, and many Sayisi Dene were still going to Churchill in summer where free traders could still contact the trappers.

By the end of the thirties, the HBC decided it would be even better to move Caribou Post further into Dene territory, and in 1941 they moved it once more, this time to Duck Lake, 128 kilometres further northwest. Gradually, more and more of the Sayisi Dene people began to go to Duck Lake for the winter months. They built log cabins scattered widely in the bush, and Duck Lake became a seasonal settlement of about 150 people.

At Duck Lake, the trading post stood at the end of a long, narrow peninsula on the southern side of the lake. Beside it were the manager's residence, and three other buildings, which served as warehouses and residences for the employees of the HBC. Next to the HBC buildings was a small Anglican church. An Anglican minister came to the settlement from time to time, but most Sundays Sandy Clipping, a Dene lay reader, conducted services.

Because the Fort Churchill Chipewyan Band did not have a reserve, they were able to continue living as they had always lived — to retain their independence, their culture, and traditions. Most of their children remained on the land with their parents. Only a few children had been sent to residential schools before the 1950s. With little contact with non-Aboriginal officials or schools, the Sayisi Dene spoke no English.

JOHN SOLOMON

It was a time when our people had a good life. We didn't have many tools. To chop wood, we used an ax and hauled it with dogs. Hunters would return late at night with their dogs, and they were cold by the time they got to their families. Every evening, you would hear the dogs when they were about to be fed. Afterwards you would hear the sound of the ax. At every dwelling, people would be chopping wood. When I used to go trapping for beaver, my feet were never dry. Sometimes we dug our feet in the snow to warm them.

BETSY ANDERSON

In Duck Lake, our people never suffered shortages. We had a lot of caribou, meat, game, fish. At the trading post, we could get tea and flour for bannock to supplement our diet.

I remember how well the people were dressed. The women would buy fancy cloth at the trading post and make the most beautiful dresses. Men wore beaded caribou-hide or moose-hide jackets. Their gloves and footwear were decorated with beads.

One beaver pelt was worth four sticks [just under two metres] of cloth — approximately fifty cents — at the trading post. One beaver pelt also bought you two scarves. It was through dealings like this that the HBC now has big department stores all over the south. When I talk about the trading post manager I get angry because they took advantage of us, not only of us the Dene, but of other Aboriginal people too.

We prepared and preserved the caribou meat so well that it lasted us through the long winter. We made lots of pemmican and dried meat. In fall when the men went on their hunting trips, they would leave supplies of caribou frozen under the snow. Anyone could go there, feel under the snow with a long stick, and take what they needed.

The well-being of children was always a priority for the community. Nobody spoke harshly to children, we never punished them, yet they were well disciplined by their parents and grandparents, raised with good values. They were always respectful towards their parents and towards elders.

The children played outside, warmly dressed in their caribou-hide jackets, pants, footwear, and mitts. When it was time to eat, the parents would call them in. In the evening, they could play for a little while and then they were told it was bedtime. They went to bed without any argument. Sometimes I heard people who lived a little further away calling their kids. Almost immediately the kids would go in. No one stayed out to run around late at night. Night time was quiet time. When I put my children to bed, it was my time to do the work that was unfinished during the day. I could prepare caribou hides. I could sew at peace. I loved that quiet time.

Adults were also respectful towards each other. We respected each other's ways. People had space.

RONNIE JOHN BUSSIDOR

I came to Duck Lake in 1941, when I was fifteen years old. A man named Anderson was the one who built the post at Duck Lake. It seemed like a time when our people were happy. They were building log cabins for themselves. It was a good life.

The store manager would bring supplies for the post by boat in summer and by dog-team in winter. The older men who were good trappers would get credit at the trading post. When I started trapping, I began to take a couple of pelts to the post from time to time.

We didn't use a lot of white man's food. We continued to live off the land with the caribou and the fish. In July and August, when the caribou herds would come, the people would go hunting. We used to trade caribou hides for ammunition and a little bit of food at the store. In summer we would go to the barren land and return to Duck Lake in the fall.

Our people walked way up into the Northwest Territories, hunting, trapping, and gathering food. In the barren lands, there used to be a place with big rapids, called *Tche Ain dh'ese*. There was a boat there. That's where people used to cross the rapids, taking turns.

When I was a young man in Duck Lake and went hunting with my dad, when we came to a place where there was a lake and animals, we would put a rock in the water in thanks. We would stand on the land, open our arms and say "Ma see cho nih" ("Thank you, nature") out loud. This is how we expressed our respect to nature, in the hope that we would be rewarded in our hunt. Everything we did was balanced with respect. There was a connection between people and nature, there was a connection between everything we did for survival.

In summer, we used to travel to Churchill and stay in tents across the river. We wouldn't think of going by boat or by plane. We travelled on foot. There was a trail used year after year, it became bare like a highway where people had made their way. There were government people, Métis, and Cree in Churchill, but our people didn't go into that community except when they had to buy something. No one ever bought liquor.

Suzanna and Artie Cheekie

On a cold October day in 1922, Betsy Anderson gave birth to her first child, a daughter. She and her husband, Thomas Ellis, named the baby Suzanna.

A few days later, when all the dry trees around the campsite had been cut down, the firewood all used up, the clan decided to move camp. Betsy put her baby on her back in a cradle-board and pulled a loaded sleigh on the snow, as did all the other woman.

When Suzanna was three years old, her father became ill and died. It was difficult for a young woman alone to raise a child, and Betsy married Albert Anderson when Suzanna was six.

Suzanna was a young girl when the HBC opened the trading post at Caribou Lake and then moved it to Duck Lake. Around this time, her family began to winter near Duck Lake. When Suzanna was eighteen, her parents told her she would be marrying a widower named Artie Cheekie, who was twenty years older than herself. The decision had been made between Suzanna's parents and Artie, a strong man, a good hunter and trapper who had a child and needed a wife. Suzanna Ellis and Artie Cheekie were married in 1940, at the little Anglican church at Duck Lake.

When Suzanna had her first baby, she and her girlfriend Caroline Thorassie —

two young mothers in their late teens — would put their babies on their backs in cradle-boards and go to the bush to collect wood. Caroline remembers that they would hang their cradle-boards on a nearby tree. Suzanna would tease her, and they would play tag, running around, chasing each other, laughing and screaming. They would take a break to nurse and change their babies, and then continue to work and to play.

Between 1941 and 1956, during the years when government decisions were dramatically and permanently changing life on the taiga and the tundra, Suzanna gave birth to eight children. She toiled ceaselessly to protect and to raise them. All her children describe her as a strong, gentle, competent woman who loved them. But her upbringing on the land hadn't prepared her for the changes that hurled her into white society. They broke her and destroyed her — as they did most of the Sayisi Dene of her generation.

An old, scratched photo shows Suzanna Cheekie with her young children in their log cabin in North River. Suzanna, a tall slender woman, is unsmiling and serene. She looks straight into the camera.

CAROLINE YASSIE

When my mom and dad were living in Duck Lake, they were both young, just beginning to raise a young family. They were healthy and strong, spiritually, physically, and mentally. They both worked hard.

My dad was elected chief when he was in his thirties or forties. He was a strong man with a powerful voice for his people — he carried himself with pride and dignity. He was not afraid to speak his mind. He had the respect of his people.

My dad's first wife had died when their son Sandy Cheekie was a little boy. A couple of years later, my dad married my mom, Suzanna Cheekie.

As far back as I can remember, my mom was working hard to survive and to raise her children. Life was always a struggle. She raised us mostly on her own on the land because my dad was often away hunting or trapping, and doing his duties as chief. [Artie Cheekie was chief between 1945 and 1960.] My mom had this little gun, a small .22. She would go out to hunt ptarmigans. She would snare rabbits and make rabbit stew. She would clean the rabbit skin, dry it, cut it in strips, and weave it to make a rabbit-fur blanket and pillows. Then she would make a cover for them out of flannel or cotton. She also made rabbit-fur liners for slippers and for kids' mukluks. When she finished her work for the day, she would put the kids to bed and then she would sew into the wee hours of the night, working with caribou hides, sewing the beadwork on. I used to stay up with her. I remember how I would drift off to sleep and she would say, "Don't go to sleep yet. Keep me company."

I remember how she melted bucketsful of snow to wash clothes. She checked the fish nets in the middle of the night in January. She would take the fish out of the net and then re-set the net in the freezing sub-arctic weather. She worked all the time. She was a very strong woman. When we ran out of basic white man's food — things like lard and flour — it was nothing for my mother to go out hunting and bring something back to feed us. I began to help her when I was about eight years old. I used to go out and help her get wood from the bush and haul it back on a sled. I used to cook bannock, help wash clothes and baby-sit. My mom even began to teach me how to sew.

My mom was always gentle and kind to me. She never spoke harshly. She used to tell me funny stories, laugh with me. My dad was the same way. He would try to do whatever I wanted. He made me a little play house out of canvas. It had a little stove inside it, with stove pipes and even a meat rack above the stove. My dad used to tease me and say to my mom, "This kid is driving me crazy, she is so bossy," and they would both laugh.

I remember a fall evening just before freeze-up, when my uncle Johnny Anderson and Thomas Duck came for a visit. My uncle Johnny Anderson always had a guitar with him wherever he went, even on long trips. He would play and sing in the light of a kerosene lamp. This time, they had brought us store-bought food. It was like a party, and just at that time my dad also returned home from his hunting trip. He brought a lot of caribou meat home with him. Everyone was happy. My dad gave meat to Johnny and Thomas to take home with them.

When I was eight years old, my mother had to go to The Pas to have a baby. She was gone for months, and I had to help my dad look after the younger kids. After a long time, someone came to our house and said, "Your mother is back." I didn't want to leave my little brother home alone, so I put him on my back and carried him to meet my mother. When my mother saw me with my brother on my back, she began to cry. When we got home, she said to me, "You are never going to work like that again."

In 1951, when I was ten years old, I was sent out to a hospital to get treatment for tuberculosis. From the hospital, government people sent me to residential school. The next time I saw my parents, I was sixteen years old; their lives were changing.

North River

While one group of Sayisi Dene formed a kind of seasonal settlement around Duck Lake, another group, who had been used to trading at Churchill and who may have been the descendants of the Homeguard Chipewyan, moved during the 1930s towards the estuary of North Knife River, about forty kilometres northwest of Churchill. In the mid-thirties, a free trader from Churchill named Art Anderson established a trading post there.[10] From then on, several Sayisi Dene families began to winter at North River. Some also went to Churchill every summer to work at the port and the railway. The family of Charlie Kithithee was among the people who camped at North River.

CHARLIE KITHITHEE

The land and the people were one. That was the secret of our life. We hunted and trapped, and everyone was able to feed their families. There were caribou, moose, rabbits, ptarmigans, and fish. There was food everywhere, one just had to go out into the bush and hunt for it. The land always provided for us. This is how the creator looked after us. He put animals onto our land so that we could provide for our people.

In late spring, the ice would break up on the river. That's when the people would travel on foot or on dogsled to Churchill, and they would camp close to there for a month or two. You could see rows of tents along the shoreline or on top of the higher grounds. The Sayisi Dene who were scattered all over the North and who wintered around Duck Lake and Caribou Lake met there to visit each other, trade their furs, and pick up supplies.

In the fall, our people would pack their gear and get ready for the trip back to North River. People would be taking down their tents and packing all their belongings, making packs for the dogs to carry on their backs. There would be a lot of excitement in the air.

When we reached North River, then we had to get ready for the fall hunt. We would send out scouts to look for caribou. When a hunter saw caribou tracks, he let other hunters know the herd was near, by burning moss to make smoke signals. Families would go out onto the barren lands to prepare the meat for the winter. Around freeze-up, the men would make caches to store the meat. Women made dry meat by the bundles. Nothing was wasted. Then the people would travel back to North River with our winter supplies. Once we were back, the men would get ready for the trapping season.

The men in the community spent most of the winter at their trap lines. The women stayed behind with the children and the elders. They didn't run short of food while the men were gone because there were a lot of rabbits, ptarmigans, and fish. Women used to set fish nets and take them out and re-set them. My mother and aunts used to do this all the time. As a young boy, I used to help them set the nets on the lake.

Just before Christmas, the men who went to the trap lines returned to the community. It was a such a festive time. Our people would come together to celebrate. In those days, there was no such thing as alcohol, it was not part of our lives. Métis people, unlike the Treaty people, were free to use alcohol, but we were not allowed to use it, and the Métis respected that. There were no laws, no orders from anybody — we just understood that this was not for us.

We enjoyed each other's company, we had fun. There were many young women, but the most beautiful, I thought, were Mina Jones and Emma Powderhorn. They were dressed in the traditional style of the Sayisi Dene women, they wore colourful dresses and beaded moccasin wrap-arounds. The dances would start before Christmas, and the people would dance right through the Christmas holidays until the new year. For us young men and women it was a very happy time. We didn't have snowmobiles, but we had our way of getting all the food we needed for our Christmas feast. We sure didn't need outsiders to give us food. There was a lot of food. Our homes were small, neat, clean, and warm. We looked after ourselves and our families with a lot of love.

I remember that after the Second World War the trading post brought in something we hadn't seen until then: record players that you could wind. For the first time, we heard music that was different from our drum songs. In the early evening I remember hearing the sound of this new music coming out of some houses. It sounded wonderful. We would be outside, playing on the ice, and the music would come spilling out to us. It has stayed in my ears, and to this day I love listening to Hank Williams.

"Preserved at all Costs"

The Second World War changed the face of the Canadian North. In 1941, when the United States entered the war, the Canadian Northwest became an important strategic zone for the American armed forces. Churchill turned into a huge military centre, and the United States Air Force built Fort Churchill, a massive military base. Thousands of American troops came into the North, disrupting wildlife and changing social relations.

After the war, the Canadian government took over the military base in Churchill and used it for its own arctic military exercises. At the height of the Cold War, the Americans built a defence lab there, which became a communications and transportation centre for the Central Arctic. Later, the National Research Council and NASA funded a rocket research range on the same site.

By the time the Second World War came to an end, ideas about resource conservation and "scientific wildlife management" among people farther south began to pose a serious threat to the Dene's access to food resources across the Canadian Northwest. Ottawa had become convinced that every major species of fur-bearing animal was threatened, and officials blamed Aboriginal over-hunting. The approaches and solutions that these officials used would often disrupt the lives of the Aboriginal people. Policies were made by administrators who often had little knowledge of northern ecology and little sympathy for Aboriginal rights. Eventually, restrictions on hunting and fishing became a major issue across the Canadian North.[1]

This new interest in conserving wildlife corresponded with another change in Canadians' attitudes towards the North. During the post-war years, many southern Canadians began to learn a little about the geology of northern Canada. They knew that the land was rich with mineral and oil deposits — and maybe even gold! The North now held a new promise for the south — it became a new source of fascination and hope for prosperity. The Government of Canada was eager to open up the vast Canadian sub-arctic to mining and hydro-electric development.

The provincial government shared Ottawa's concerns about the threats to fur-bearing animals. In 1946, the Government of Manitoba introduced registered trap lines and severely restricted the movement of trappers, thus unintentionally forcing trappers to over-harvest a small area before the animals had time to reproduce. The government's system ran counter to the traditional Sayisi Dene method of conserving wildlife by trapping over a very large area in a location one year, then leaving it fallow the next year to let the animal population grow, when they would harvest another location. But provincial authorities did not understand the cyclical nature of the populations of fur-bearing animals. They resented the Sayisi Dene's use of such huge spaces.[2]

The Dene's role in the fur trade was coming to an end. Fur prices had tumbled while the cost of ammunition and other goods went up. The profits of the HBC were continuing to go down, and by the end of the 1940s the Company decided to close many northern trading posts. The post at Duck Lake was one of them.

For the Sayisi Dene, trapping for furs had never become as important as hunting caribou for food, clothing, and shelter. When the trapping economy faltered, they had to go without tea and tobacco and a few other consumer goods. Some people went to Churchill to look for work at the port, the army base, and CN rail.[3] But as long as they could hunt caribou, as long as they could fish, their survival was not threatened.

In 1947, federal and provincial wildlife officials began to survey caribou populations across the country. Based on aerial and ground surveys, they estimated the caribou population between Hudson Bay and the Mackenzie Valley to be around 670,000. Six years later, in the spring of 1955, officials and wildlife scientists repeated the aerial surveys and this time estimated the caribou population to be only 277,000. This was an alarming decline of over 400,000 animals! After analyzing and dismissing various possible causes of this loss (such as disease, scarcity of food, forest fires, drowning), scientists concluded that two culprits were destroying the caribou: wolves and hunters.[4]

In the fall of 1955, a small group of officials from the Manitoba Department of Natural Resources went on a northern expedition to check trap lines and do wolf and caribou counts from the air. An information writer for the Department of

Industry and Commerce went along with them. Their Norseman aircraft, which was equipped with floats, had engine trouble and had to land on Nejanilini Lake. As the plane descended, the officials saw about two dozen men and boys in canoes, near the rapids. They were harpooning caribou as the herd tried to cross the narrows. By the time the officials landed, the hunters had disappeared, but they had left hundreds of dead and dying animals on the shores of the narrows. The information writer happened to have a Roloflex camera with her. The officials of the Department of Natural Resources asked her to take photographs. She did.

A month later, on October 13, 1955, officials from the provincial game departments of Ontario, Manitoba, and Saskatchewan, and the federal departments of Northern Affairs and Citizenship and Immigration, met in Saskatoon to set up the Caribou Conservation Committee. Both the federal and provincial governments had been alarmed by the results of the caribou survey, and they were meeting to plan a strategy to deal with the "caribou crisis." At that meeting, J.D. Robertson of the Manitoba Game Branch complained about the Sayisi Dene's hunting methods. He had photos to prove his case.

> The Chipewyan people were major offenders in wastage of caribou. He showed the meeting coloured slides taken the previous month at Duck Lake in northern Manitoba. There a total of sixteen hunters had shot or harpooned about 750 caribou, most of which had been left where they fell or were washed ashore. The same situation might be duplicated in other places from Churchill to Brochet wherever the Chipewyans live. In most of this area the dogs were fed almost exclusively on caribou even though fish could be obtained. Mr. Daggett of Indian Affairs Branch corroborated Mr. Robertson's statements.[5]

Next spring, the photo of the caribou carcasses taken by the Department of Industry and Commerce information writer accompanied an article entitled "The Caribou Crisis," which appeared in the *Beaver* magazine. The article was written by Dr. A.W.F. Banfield, chief mammalogist for the Canadian Wildlife Service and a leader of the caribou surveys. Banfield identified wasteful hunting as the central reason for the decline in caribou population and dramatically described the "scenes of carnage. . . . Orgies of killing still take place at several crossing points where caribou are speared from canoes or kayaks as they cross lakes in crowded ranks. Each year thousands of caribou carcasses are abandoned — their bloated bodies crowding the shores of northern lakes whose waters flowed red a few days before."[6]

At a time when wildlife officials had decided that the caribou were in serious decline, and when they had identified Aboriginal over-hunting as the main cause of that decline, the photographs of the caribou hunt at Duck Lake had focussed their attention on the Sayisi Dene.

The scientists were pointing to the carcasses left on the shores of Duck Lake as evidence of wastage, yet the Dene had been following their centuries-old method of survival. For them, leaving carcasses to be buried under the winter snow was a time-honoured, reasonable way of storing some meat, in a land where winters were long and harsh and where the people could never be sure of enough food for their families.

For hundreds of years, the Sayisi Dene had watched and followed the caribou herds. The caribou were central to their way of life. If the caribou were in decline, the Sayisi Dene would have suffered more than anyone else. The people at Duck Lake had not seen a drop in the number of caribou migrating south. They had no reason to be worried, no reason to change their centuries-old pattern of hunting. They were not aware of the government's concerns about the depletion of the herd.

Conservation Committee reports show that government officials talked about "educating" the Dene. But there's no record of anyone ever asking the Sayisi Dene why they killed so many caribou at one time and left the carcasses on the shores. There's no evidence that anyone attempted to persuade them to hunt differently.

By the middle of the twentieth century, "scientific resource management" had become the dominant approach towards the Canadian North and its people. Unfortunately, this approach was insensitive to the traditional life of the people in the North. In 1949, one Indian Affairs official expressed it with regret: "The Indians all were worried about the restriction to killing caribou and other animals for food. We sympathize with them. The mammalogists who have stated that certain wild life must be preserved at all costs fail to take into account the human element, I fear."[7]

The scientists and officials who failed to consider the "human element" also accepted the widespread belief that Aboriginal people needed to assimilate, that their traditional life had no value in the modern world. More than ever before, Canadians assumed it was time for "Native peoples" to settle down, earn wages, and become part of the general population. Most people didn't know much about the history or culture of any Aboriginal group, but they took the superiority of the "white" way of life for granted. In more southerly regions of the country, Aboriginal children were being scooped up and sent to residential schools so they could learn new ways of living, and assimilate. In the far North, many children were still in the bush, uneducated. Health care was also a problem — polio and tuberculosis were rampant in northern Aboriginal communities. The well-meaning officials of the Department of Indian Affairs saw only one solution to these problems: to integrate "the Indians" into "white" society.

THE RELOCATION

*I*n 1951, the Government of Canada adopted a new Indian act, which openly aimed to assimilate all Aboriginal peoples into Canadian society."[1] Both the federal and the provincial governments assumed that integrating Aboriginal peoples into the wage economy was desirable and inevitable. This attitude provided the backdrop for the displacement of the Sayisi Dene and for their suffering in the second half of the twentieth century.

During the early 1950s, two other factors emerged to seal the fate of the Sayisi Dene. They were no longer needed in the fur trade. And even more important, their traditional caribou hunt had become unacceptable to conservation officials.

In the early 1950s, officials of the Department of Indian Affairs, the HBC, and the Manitoba Department of Natural Resources jointly set in motion the series of events that changed the lives of the Sayisi Dene. The paper trail documenting the discussions and decisions that were taking place in Ottawa and Winnipeg is sparse, broken, confusing, and even contradictory. But it does make clear that the process to move the Dene from Duck Lake had started long before anyone told the Dene what was in store for them.

As early as 1953, plans were being developed to move the Sayisi Dene out of their traditional lands. That year, the manager of the HBC Central Post Division in Winnipeg wrote to one of his superiors: "Mr. Gowans, Superintendent of Indian Affairs, Ilford, was in to see me this morning. He advises that an appropriation has been authorised by Ottawa to move the Duck Lake band to the North Knife River at a point approximately forty air miles [about sixty-five kilometres by air] from Churchill."[2]

The next document to mention the relocation is a letter from an HBC official to the director, Department of Citizenship and Immigration at the Indian Affairs Branch in Ottawa, on June 28, 1956:

> This will confirm that we will be closing our post at Caribou in September of this year for the reasons discussed with you during my visit last month. . . . Over the past five years there has been a steady decrease in the business at Caribou, and over the same period the number of trappers has decreased from twenty-nine to fifteen. . . . Our representative has discussed the problem with your Mr. Nield and the latter has been emphatic in stating that your Department would like to move the Indians from Caribou nearer to Churchill in an effort to improve their lot. The Plan, I believe, would be to build them houses, etc., which is impracticable as long as they remain at Caribou where their situation is so poor.[3]

In July, the Acting Supervisor of Indian Affairs for the region, R.D. Ragan, wrote to the clerk in charge at the Nelson River Indian Agency in Ilford, telling him that the HBC was pulling out of Duck Lake and, by so doing, creating "a terrific problem for this office and we have no alternative but to attempt to move these Indians out of the area. . . . It is going to mean that we will have to move very swiftly." In the same letter, Ragan stated that he would meet with "the Indians [and] . . . attempt to persuade them to move to a location where they can be looked after."[4]

On July 23 and 24, Ragan did meet with the "Duck Lake Band" to pay treaty money and to discuss "their plight" and the "intended move." Since the Dene spoke no English, and Ragan and his officials spoke no Dene, a real discussion was out of the question. Nevertheless, Ragan wrote in a departmental memo on July 27, 1956, that the band had agreed to move to North River to join those who were already wintering there: "After a very full discussion it was unanimously and amicably agreed by the Duck Lake Band still at this Post that they would move to the mouth of the North River. A part of their Band live at this point in hovels during the winter and it is the only logical place for those remaining at Caribou to move to."[5]

In the same letter, Ragan also alluded to the reasons for the planned move: "The Hudson's Bay Company post is closing in September and it is imperative that we evacuate these Indians not later than the end of August. The large caribou trek reaches this area early in September and *we feel that we must have them evacu-*

ated before that time or they will wish to remain for the kill which might upset all our plans" [emphasis added].[6]

Most of the Sayisi Dene who were at the meeting with R.D. Ragan are dead, and today, no one can attest to what was offered, what was agreed to, what was promised. In view of the immense communication problems faced by both sides, what Ragan meant by a "full discussion" is anyone's guess.

> The people from the Department of Natural Resources started coming around and they implied we were slaughtering the caribou. When we had Treaty Days in July 1956, there was a meeting in a tent. I wasn't inside but I stood outside for a while and heard that the move was mentioned. It was said we would be closer to medical services if we were moved near Churchill. The Hudson's Bay manager never said anything. I think it was the people from the Department of Natural Resources and from the Department of Indian Affairs who wanted to move us. . . . Artie Cheekie, who was the chief at that time, spoke at that meeting. He said, "Our people are here because the caribou come here. There are plenty of fish on these connecting lakes and that's why this trading post was built here, to be near us. What is there for us to live on in Churchill? (John Solomon)

> When the people were informed that they would be moved, many of them didn't understand the reasons behind the move, or what was supposed to happen to them. It wasn't what the people wanted, but their wishes weren't taken into consideraton. (Betsy Anderson)

Ragan's letter mentions that, at the meeting, government officials promised Dene families that they would provide them with materials necessary to construct log cabins: "All heads of families promised the writer during our meetings that immediately on landing at North River they would construct log houses, and I, in return promised to provide the necessary roofs, floors, doors and windows for these homes."[7]

On August 10, 1956, Ragan received authorization from the Indian Affairs Branch to "move the Indians and their belongings by air to Churchill." He sent a telegram to the post manager at Little Duck Lake confirming August 17 as the date for the move.[8] The plan was to move the band by air to Churchill and to let the people camp there until they could be taken to North Knife River by boat.

On the afternoon of August 17, 1956, a Canso amphibious military aircraft landed on the waters of Duck Lake. Four men came out of the aircraft: the Indian agent, two officials of the Department of Indian Affairs, and the pilot. They told the people that today was the day, the people were going to be moved, that they should pack up their belongings and get into the plane. Before long, everyone was rushing around trying to gather their things. Some took along their tents. Many people didn't know what to do about their traps, their toboggans, their log cabins. They left them. In a couple of hours, the military aircraft took off with fifty-eight people and seventy-three dogs on board. After a one-hour flight, as the afternoon sun was going down, the aircraft delivered its living cargo to the shores of the Churchill River, near Hudson Bay.

Stewart Yassie was only five years old at the time. He was living at Duck Lake with his aunt, Nancy French, and her husband, Sandy French. He remembers that flight:

> As the plane started taking off, the dogs were all fighting and howling and everything and when the plane took off, when you haven't ridden a plane for a lifetime, you know how it is, you want to puke and that. That was the reason why I remember that trip because all the kids were throwing up and I remember that I didn't. That plane stunk so much inside because there was dogs there that were throwing up and they were fighting and everything and those dogs were working dogs and you don't go bathing working dogs for anything and you can imagine how the smell was in that plane. That's why I remember that trip.

Stewart Yassie also remembers the truck that came to pick them up in late evening:

> There was an old army truck that came there and they boarded us on there — they just boarded us on there just like cattle and we didn't know where we were going. We weren't used to the environment or any ways of white man's society so I remember they drove us from — they used to call it camp — from camp to the point where they were just building the Harbours Board. And they dropped us off right there, right at the point, right at the shoreline, just sand and rock, that's all. Imagine, to come from a good environment and then you end up in a place where there's just rocks and sand. When we got out there our people didn't have much, some people were lucky that they brought their tents, so the evening came and the people that had some tents there, they managed to scrounge up some two-by-four — you can't find no trees standing in Churchill, so some two-by-four or some twigs or something they pitched it up and they were, say, from one, two, three families in one little, say, ten-by-eight tent. That's where we were dropped, we had nothing, we didn't even know where to turn.

John Solomon was thirty years old in 1956. He is one of the few Sayisi Dene who were adults at the time of the move and who are still alive:

> The plane came with three white people plus the pilot. They said they came to move the people. The people never replied. We took whatever we could with us, we left behind our traps, our toboggans, our cabins, and we got into that plane. When we got out in Churchill, there were no trees. The wind was blowing sand on everything. We didn't know what to do next. We couldn't do anything there. We couldn't go trapping. We couldn't set a net. There was nothing to hunt. We were in a desperate state. We had nothing to live on.

Some of the Sayisi Dene were in Churchill at the time and remember seeing the arrival of the people. Betsy Anderson and her second husband, Albert Anderson, were in Churchill because Betsy was receiving medical care for her injured back. She witnessed the arrival of the Sayisi Dene at Churchill that day:

> I remember when the people were brought to Churchill, my husband and I watched them being unloaded off the plane at the shores of Hudson Bay. "This is a bad, bad thing for our people," we said. "Somebody's making a great mistake. From here on, they will be suffering. They are not prepared for this." There were no houses for them anywhere. The winter was closing in. I was very saddened by what was happening. I felt, From now on, there'll be nothing but disaster for our people.

Charlie Kithithee, twenty years old at the time, was working at the army base in Churchill, along with his older brother Alex and another Sayisi Dene man, Johnny Oman. He also witnessed the arrival of the Sayisi Dene from Duck Lake:

> We were working at the airport. We were outside, doing casual labour, when the plane landed and the people were unloaded. The plane was a huge aircraft with a round belly. It landed and the people came out one by one. I remember the children crying and the few dogs yelping to get free. Eventually everything and everyone was unloaded and put on a big truck and driven down into the town. They were all taken to the point at Cape Merry. There, the people were dumped to fend for themselves on the shores of Hudson Bay. Winter was closing in. Some of the people set up their tents, and some made makeshift shelters for themselves. One of the tents stood out because you could see the shadows of the people who were sitting inside. Already, the feeling of hopelessness was in the air. There was no laughter, no joy, only dead silence. Even the dogs were not moving. The feeling just hung over the people like death.

The people stayed on the beach on the shores of the Churchill River for three weeks, waiting for the next move. In the sub-arctic, late August brought the onset of winter, with rain and hail and sharp winds. The adults spoke no English. They didn't know what was going on or what was going to happen.

Less than a month after the Sayisi Dene had been moved from Duck Lake, their chief, Artie Cheekie, attended a meeting in The Pas, with R.D. Ragan, Colonel Fortier, Deputy Minister, Department of Citizenship and Immigration, and other officials from Ottawa. As the other chiefs spoke about trap-line registrations and reserve boundaries, Chief Cheekie raised his concerns about the recent move of his people. The minutes of that meeting are just brief summaries of the discussion. But it's clear from them that Artie Cheekie and the Sayisi Dene knew that the relocation would be disastrous and that he was straightforward in telling this to Indian Affairs:

> *Artie Cheekie, Chief Churchill:* Recently band moved to Churchill and found move unsatisfactory, too near town and would like to move to another place with fish and

game. Maybe all right for one to three years but after that place will be depleted and no good for future generations.

Col. Fortier: Move just taken place and we believe to a better area than before, on road to caribou, fishing area available next to them. Move only temporary, but if they would co-operate and stay for some time, we are going to have an agent there who will work with the Chief and it is only after a year that the chief and ourselves will be in a position to know if place is suitable or not.

Chief Cheekie: Glad arrangements made to study this move — know land will not be suitable for my band.[9]

It was mid-September when two Peterhead boats arrived in Churchill to take the Sayisi Dene to North River. They made two trips over a week. The relocation was accomplished:

The people were dumped in Churchill with no way to fend for themselves. There was no shelter. The people set up tents along the shores of Hudson Bay. It was cold. Then, a barge was brought from the CN and most of our people were taken up to North River and they were left there. That winter, the people lived in tents in North River. Some built log cabins. (Ronnie John Bussidor)

In late fall, when winter was coming, most of the people were taken towards North River, and dumped at the point called Sand Island, just before North River. The Indian Affairs agent had arranged to give people lumber to build houses with, but along the way most of it was lost or damaged. And besides, the people didn't have any equipment to build houses with. They had no hammers, no nails. All in all, the poor planning by Indian Affairs in relocating a whole community of people on such short notice had disturbed everyone terribly. Everything fell apart right from the start. The food supply was not adequate. The people eventually left Sand Island on their own as they knew they would not be able to survive through the winter in those conditions. Some headed back to North River and some went to Churchill. Everyone felt displaced. The people couldn't adapt to this strange way of living, not knowing what was going to happen the next day. They just drifted like lost souls. It took a few years for our people to start drinking alcohol. (Charlie Kithithee)

I also remember the time we were moved to Churchill. When our elders say that the people were dumped on the shores of Hudson Bay, they are telling the truth. Some families didn't have tents for shelter, and they had young children, but they were left like that. As the winter set in we had no other way but to live in a canvas tent for the whole winter. My dad eventually built a shack with scrap lumber across the Churchill River where some people were living. We would live there in the winter and come across to the town and summer at the point, Cape Merry. We had a homemade stove made out of a forty-five-gallon gas tank. People didn't own proper woodstoves in those days. (Mary Yassie)

According to Charlie Kithithee, before the relocation of the Duck Lake Sayisi Dene, there were five families staying at North River. When the Duck Lake people arrived, the population more than doubled. The wildlife and firewood in the area couldn't sustain the community. Without caribou, the people had no winter clothing or shelter. They couldn't feed their dogs, so they couldn't go trapping.

The government had intended to build cabins at North River for those who were relocated. But transporting the building materials became a problem. "A few supplies of tar-paper, roofing and lumber were brought and left on the shore. High tide came and washed them away. People retrieved a few of these and built log cabins with their axes from the stunted logs of North River."[10] Some people took shelter in abandoned dilapidated cabins that had belonged to an independent trapper. The newcomers survived that winter with difficulty. Yet, in Winnipeg, R.D. Ragan wrote in a memo on November 22, 1956, that, as far as he was aware at the moment, "all Indians [were] more or less comfortably housed."[11] In the spring of 1957, North River flooded its banks, destroying makeshift cabins and other belongings. The people had nowhere to go, except Churchill: "That spring, people started going back to Churchill. They went back and forth between North River and Churchill for another year. Some people began to build shacks in Churchill on DOT [Department of Transport] Hill and 'the point'. That's when the white men began to see our people living there and became concerned. But the people had been moved and there had been nothing for them" (Ronnie John Bussidor).

In 1956, the total Sayisi Dene population was between 250 and 300. Fifty-eight people had been picked up by plane on the day of the relocation from Duck Lake. Others who lived at Duck Lake were away on their trap lines, and some had gone to Churchill to trade. Several families of men working for the port and the elevator were already living in Churchill. There were also the families who regularly lived at North River. Wherever they had been at the time of the relocation from Duck Lake, the move disrupted the lives of all the Sayisi Dene. Those who were away on trap lines or away to trade on that day now had no community to return to. Those who had been wintering around North River would not be able to maintain their way of life for much longer. And those who already lived in Churchill would eventually share the fate of those who were displaced.

In the summer of 1957, after the people had been relocated from Duck Lake to Churchill, Caroline Yassie (Ila's older sister) returned home from residential school to visit her parents. The Sayisi Dene were moving back and forth between Churchill and North River, unable to hunt enough caribou for food or for shelter. Her parents, Artie and Suzanna Cheekie, were in Churchill.

CAROLINE YASSIE

When I returned for my visit, my parents were living in a tent across the river from Churchill. They would live there in the summer and return to North River for the winter. Because we were not allowed to speak our language in residential school, I was no longer able to speak Dene. I had lost my language.

When I arrived at the Churchill train station, my granny Betsy and my uncle Jimmy were there to meet me. They took me back to their tent, which was close to the railway tracks. Ronnie John Bussidor walked over to where my parents were living to let them know that I had returned to Churchill from school. As soon as my father found out that I was back, he came across on a boat to pick me up. When my dad walked into my granny's tent, he was so happy to see me, he held me in his arms and cried. He was crying because a few years before, my little sister Marjorie had been sent away to a tuberculosis sanatorium. She was only seven years old when she died in that hospital. My father had loved that little girl in a very special way, and when she died a part of him died with her. Her body was never returned to be buried on our land, which added to his grief. These are the reasons why he was overjoyed to see me.

We left that same day, and spent the night at my uncle Joe Bighead's house across the river. Early the next morning we finally got ready to complete the last part of my journey. It was a beautiful summer morning. The sun was bright and hot. Like many other families who drifted back and forth between Churchill and North River, my parents were, at the time, also camping halfway to North River at a good fishing spot. My father was carrying my luggage as we walked home to where my mother was. We got there in the early morning, therefore most of the people were still asleep. When we walked into my parents' tent, my mother was so happy to see me, she cried and held me for a long time. It was hard for her to let me go, she couldn't believe that I had come home.

In those days, Indian Affairs decided which children were to be sent away to residential school. I had just been back for about one week when they told me that I would have to attend summer school in Brandon, Manitoba. I had to separate from my family once again. I had no choice but to attend this summer school, so once again I left home for school. There they taught us how to cook and sew, and just basic home economics. At the end of August 1957 I returned home, and after just a few days with my family I was told that I had to go back to residential school in Prince Albert, Saskatchewan. I had been so lonely when I was away from my family that I didn't want to go back to school. I made up my mind that I wasn't going back, and the rest of the students left without me. That was the last time that I ever went to school.

In the fall we packed up our belongings and headed back to North River. My mother carried my youngest sister in a cradle-board on her back. This was the way babies were carried in those days. We all had to carry something. Even the dogs had packs strapped onto their backs. It was about thirty to forty miles inland from the Hudson Bay coast. The Kithithee family travelled with us. When we reached North River, we spent the night at my aunt and uncle's place. From there we walked up the river to a large log cabin my father had just built. I remember how nice it was inside this new log cabin. I loved the smell of the freshly cut wood. We moved into the cabin although it wasn't completely finished. My father had to go on a hunting trip to get a supply of fresh caribou meat for the winter.

While he was away, a 'flu epidemic swept the community. Most of the people got sick. Most of us were bedridden and too weak to put wood in the stove or prepare a meal. We had no medicine, and there were no doctors to help us. The cold weather had set in, and the river was freezing up. The only two who never caught this 'flu were my little brother Fred and my little sister Sarah. They were only six and seven years old. They gathered wood and kept the fire going and made tea for all the sick families. My father came home and found us all sick in bed except for Fred and Sarah. With the help of some men, my father finished the log cabin and got it ready for the winter. From his hunting trip my father brought home dried caribou meat, but we were too sick to eat. I was recovering from this 'flu but was still feeling very weak. My mother was still too sick to get out of bed, so I had to get up and change the baby's diaper and feed the kids. After more than a month we slowly recovered.

Since most of the kids my age were away at residential school in the winter, I used to go sliding with my little brother and sister and other kids just to pass time. Under the bright moonlight, you could hear the sound of the children laughing and squealing as they slid down the steep hill. I was amongst them. We had so much fun playing that although it was winter we never felt the cold.

In the following winter [1958-59] we were living in Churchill in a tent. I remember that it was very cold even though we had a large woodstove. My mother had to pack snow around the edges of our tent in order to keep out the wind. Just to keep warm we had to keep the fire going all night. During those cold winter nights my mother would keep the baby's milk warm by putting the bottle inside this little pouch, which she then placed under her shirt next to her skin. The pouch was made out of caribou hide with the fur on the inside. When my mother had to feed the baby in the middle of the night, the milk would be warm.

I always helped my mother look after the kids. If my little brothers and sisters were in an accident I would give them first-aid treatment. One time, one of my little sisters got a piece of broken glass in her eye. I came home and found her lying in bed crying. I lifted her up and saw that her eye was bleeding. She told me that there was a piece of glass in her eye. I managed to remove it by placing my tongue on the glass.

ILA BUSSIDOR

I was born in the army hospital at Fort Churchill in the spring of 1955. As a toddler I lived in North River. It was called *Dist'cha* by my people and was about forty miles inland from the Hudson Bay coast.

We lived in a one-room log cabin facing the river. My father's sister and her husband, Joe and Jessie Bighead, lived further down on a peninsula. There were other cabins around us. I remember that there were trees everywhere. I can still remember the inside of our cabin. In the centre of our cabin was a woodstove also used for cooking, and there was always a large kettle with water on top of the stove. My parents' homemade bed stood against one wall, and my little baby sister's swing was hanging above it. My brother and sister's bed was smaller and was on the opposite side of the room. My mother kept our place neat and clean.

There is one memory that keeps coming back to me from this time. It's a winter night and I am lying in my bed. I am drifting in and out of sleep. Our house is very warm and quiet. The room glows in the light of a kerosene lamp. There is a kettle on top of the stove, and inside the kettle the water is boiling and the steam is coming out of its spout. My mother walks up to the stove and puts wood into it. I can hear the water boiling in the kettle and the wood burning inside the stove. Everything is quiet and calm. My mother's presence reassures me that I am safe, very loved and protected. I drift back to sleep.

My mother was a beautiful woman. She was gentle and kind and always very loving towards us. She never raised her voice at us. I don't remember my parents ever spanking any one of us. There were eight of us in the family. My older brothers and sisters were attending residential school in the south. My early memories are more of my brother Fred, and my sisters Sarah and Marjorie. I remember sitting around the table while my mother cut out paper dolls, figures of people, dogs and sleds, out of cardboard paper from cookie or tea boxes. We would play with these paper figures for hours. She also taught us how to make dolls out of cloth.

When we were very young, my mother taught each one of us the Lord's Prayer in Dene. Every night when she put us to bed, we would all repeat the prayer as she sat with us. When we were finished, she would tuck us into bed, kiss us, and tell us not to make any more noise or the Night Spirits would hear us.

We had to respect these Spirits of the Night. They were our relatives who did not make the complete journey to the spirit world and who were like lost souls drifting in the night. If we made any noise, it would disturb and anger them. We believed that when your loved one dies you are given a time period to grieve, and during this time it is your right to grieve in any way as long as it is within this time frame. After this you have to let go and release the spirit of your loved one so that it will journey to the spirit world. Some people are not willing to let their loved ones go even in death. The Night Spirits are also crying to be set free, and the more we hold onto our grief, neither of us will ever be free. Therefore, the spirits of the deceased linger in the night, always near us. Until we go through the process of grieving in the way we are supposed to, they will always be lost and forever drifting in the night. This grieving process is something that is vital to healing the soul. If it is taken care of in the right way, the spirits of the living and the dead are balanced.

My father was a tall, handsome man. He was always well dressed, and he usually wore a beaded jacket made out of caribou hide. The hood of the jacket was trimmed with wolf fur. His moccasins and gloves were also made out of caribou hide and beautifully decorated with beads. He was a leader and carried himself with pride and dignity.

My father spent a lot of time on the land hunting and trapping. He travelled everywhere on a dog-team. The sleds and harnesses were usually decorated with bells and coloured ribbons. Caribou antlers were sometimes used as an anchor for the dog-team. The sound of the bells could be heard for miles. This is how my mother would know that my father was coming back even though he was a few miles away. My mother would call us and tell us that our father was coming, and we would all run outside to await his arrival, even in winter. I remember how my father would carry me in his arms and hold me close to him. When his arms got tired he would try to set me down on the bed or chair and I refused to let go of him, so he had no choice but to continue carrying me around. I remember his hugs and kisses and how he would tickle me with his whiskers. I was his baby girl. Memories of this special love from my father are something that will stay within my soul forever.

My mother worked all the time. In the winter she would haul snow and melt it in buckets on top of the stove. Once the water was ready, she would do the laundry by hand in a large aluminum tub with a washboard. Even in the winter she would have to hang most of the clothes outside on the clothesline.

Preserving caribou meat was another of her chores. The way she made dried meat was by cutting the meat into thin strips and hanging it on the meat rack above the stove to dry. Most of this dried meat would then be made into pemmican. She pounded it until it was a powder, into which she would mix grease and wild red berries. Then she would shape it into small balls, place them into a bag, and store them outside on the meat rack. Prepared like this, the meat would never go bad. In the summer time all this would be done outside in a smoke house, which was shaped like a teepee. My mother would also tan caribou hides in order to make mukluks and mittens. She would use a tool made out of caribou bone to scrape all the flesh off the hide and then cut the hair off and re-scrape it. Once the hide was clean, she would rinse the blood off it with water. She would then soak the hide in luke-warm water with ground-up caribou brains to soften it. And then she would hang it outside to dry. The next step would be to bring it in and soak it again and wring it out until all the water was gone. It would then be stretched over and over again until it was completely dried like a cloth. And then it would be smoked. Once all this was done, the smoked hide would then be cut into patterns for mukluks and mitts or jackets and sewn together. This was how most of our clothes were made. Since my mother was known as one of the best seamstresses, she was often called upon by other women to sew clothes.

Like most women of that time, my mother knew how to handle a rifle. I remember how she would go out into the bush to hunt ptarmigans. When she came back, her sack would be full. She would then clean and pluck it and then either boil or fry the ptarmigan. To this day I haven't eaten anything as good as fried ptarmigan. It was my favourite food. I don't remember ever being hungry in those days. In the winter, my mother also had to set, check, and reset the fish net on a daily basis. We kids would be standing around watching my mother as she pulled the net out of the ice hole. I remember watching all the fish wiggling around in the net. These are some of the things my mother had to do to survive on the land. She was a hard worker.

Outside our cabin we had a high wooden rack on which we would store caribou meat. In the spring time my father would set small traps for the birds that would come to pick at the meat. I remember how one spring day my sister Sarah climbed up onto the rack, sprang one of these traps, and got her fingers caught in it. When my father heard her scream, he ran out of the house and released her hand from the trap.

I remember playing outside on moonlit nights sliding down a big hill with all the other kids. One night my brother Fred made me sit on the sled alone to slide down the hill by myself. Just when the sled started picking up speed, there was a dog crossing my path. I collided with the dog, and the impact of this collision flung the dog on top of me. This frightened me so much that I started to scream. Now the dog and I are speeding down the hill, and the dog is yelping and trying to jump off unsuccessfully because the sled is going too fast. This lasted until the sled came to a stop at the bottom of the hill. The dog ran off and I remained there screaming. Although this frightened me, it must have looked so hilarious that my brother and the other kids who were standing on top of the hill were rolling over laughing. My brother came down to help me back up the hill and we all continued sliding. This is how we passed our time and always had fun.

I also remember the drum dance and the Christmas feast. The people would come together and prepare for the feast. They would bring caribou meat, fish, geese, and ptarmigans. Everyone would take part in cooking the food. Bannock was made and there would be buckets of tea and coffee. After the feast, just before the dance, we would hear the sound of the drum beat. It seemed to echo for miles and miles through the wilderness. I loved it as if I knew that sound from another life, and it would awaken our spirits.

In those days some of the people would walk to Churchill. I remember people walking in groups. Along the way, they would stop and make camp to rest and have a meal. I once asked my granny where these people were going, and she told me it must have been one of the annual trips in the spring time when they would go to Churchill to pick up supplies.

These pieces of memories are all I have left of living in *Dist'cha*.

CHURCHILL

hurchill was booming during the 1950s. The massive military operation had
become a bustling townsite with living quarters, shops, a recreation centre,
and a hospital. The town had a mixture of non-Aboriginal, Cree, Métis, and Inuit
peoples (most of whom had just moved to Churchill previously), and it had a large
transient population. Alcoholism was widespread among all residents and was becoming a problem for outlying communities.[1]

The main employer in Churchill had always been the government.[2] The non-
Aboriginal population of the town was made up of military personnel, government officials, port and elevator workers, and entrepreneurs looking for opportu-
nity in the northern frontier.

Of the Cree population, some had gone to Churchill from York Factory in the
late twenties during the construction of the port. Others had moved there after
1955, when York Factory was closed. Most of them lived in the areas called "the
Flats." The Inuit had gone there to work at the port, or to receive health care. The
federal Department of Northern Affairs had built a community called Akudlik
(Camp-20) for them between 1953 and 1955, just before the Sayisi Dene were
relocated.

Up to the time of relocation, the Sayisi Dene had been isolated from the non-Aboriginal society. They ended up on the margins of that frontier society without preparation or support. They became the lowest of the low on the social scale. None of the other people who lived in Churchill understood or was sympathetic to the Sayisi Dene.

By the summer of 1957, the families who had been air-lifted from Duck Lake had congregated on the shores of the Churchill River. Most of the Sayisi Dene who had been wintering at North River and who had been travelling to Churchill in summer to trade and to look for work also went there. They gathered on the site of their seasonal encampments and on the hillside behind the grain elevator (called DOT Hill). They lived in canvas tents and tar-paper shacks they built from materials they found in the dump, waiting for government officials to fulfill their promises.

In May 1957, the director of the Department of Health and Public Welfare in Winnipeg wrote an indignant letter to an official at the Indian Health Services Department of National Health and Welfare complaining about the "Indian squatters":

> These folk are particularly primitive in their ways and live under the most horrible sanitary conditions. They are in the eyes of our Inspector, "a serious Public Health problem." We are wondering whether informal squatting is to continue indefinitely or whether any thought has been given to the provision and development of a formal camping area. Ideally, this should be across the River mouth from the town. . . . As you know, Churchill's townsite is very much in the mind of Government these days and there is evidence that the special circumstances which obtain there may be recognised so that the beginning of a community betterment program may be undertaken.[3]

Meanwhile, the Sayisi Dene had no fuel, and not enough food. Some of them set nets in the Churchill River for whitefish. From time to time hunters went inland to look for caribou. But game wardens were determined to restrict the caribou hunt, so Indian agents reduced the ammunition made available to hunters. On November 8, 1957, a provincial conservation officer wrote the assistant Indian agent working in Churchill, asking him to prevent "caribou wastage."

> For instance, if the Indian has fifty shells he will no doubt shoot until the ammunition is gone, this will result in a large kill. The Chipewayan, it has been proven, will make these kills but if caribou are available closer home at a later date, will abandon the original kill and make a new kill at the new location. . . .
> If you could make your ammunition issuance quite small, say five shells at a time, and spread over a good period of time to prevent a build up of ammunition, it is believed it would assist a great deal in the prevention of wastage and ensure meat on hand at the same time. . . .

To further impress the matter upon you I will come to Churchill armed with literature, photos, and movies of caribou wastage that you might fully realize the situation as it has existed.[4]

The Sayisi Dene's dogs were considered a nuisance and a rabies threat, so the RCMP shot them. Without dog-teams, the Dene couldn't travel to trap lines: "What few dogs we had were either taken away or shot and so we were left with little to work with. We couldn't go very far. In our traditional territory up north, we used to travel great distances carrying food with us to keep us going while we trapped and hunted. In Churchill it was like we were imprisoned" (John Solomon).

Many of the relocated people returned to North River that winter, but they could not make a living. They came to Churchill in the summer of 1958 and stayed there.

By the summer of 1957, about 300 Sayisi Dene had congregated in Churchill. Families who had been coming to Churchill in summer since the thirties, to work for the railway and the harbour, were living in shacks made of tar paper and discarded packing cases, in an area behind the National Harbours Board elevators.[5] Now, the Duck Lake and North River groups were also scattered on the west shore of the Churchill River, on DOT Hill and in "the Point." Officials considered them all squatters.

In June 1957, the National Harbours Board decided to build an oil-storage terminal at the location of the "squatters'" shacks. The Department of National Defence asked the RCMP to formally evict fourteen "Indian" families. The people had nowhere to go. Suddenly, the issue of housing the Sayisi Dene became urgent.

On June 24, 1957, J.R. Tully, Superintendent of the Nelson River Indian Agency, wrote to R.D. Ragan describing the problems related to the eviction: "With the above in mind, I feel that now is the time for us to acquire land in the Churchill area where the Indians from North River can pitch their tents in the summer while seeking summer employment and also where the majority of the Indians who live at Churchill twelve months of the year can take up residence and not be called squatters."[6]

Further down in the same letter, Tully says, "The Indians have no objection whatsoever, to being moved to a new site. Chief Artie Cheekie and his two councillors, John Duck and Peter Bussidor advise that they will be very happy to have a parcel of ground in Churchill that the Indians can call their own and not be branded as squatters."[7]

Officials wrote back and forth to each other, all agreeing that "the Indians" desperately needed housing. They considered a series of options, from providing survival cabins to selling houses to "the Indians" to buying land for a tent reserve.

Knowing full well that the Sayisi Dene had lived in a bartering system with the HBC for more than 200 years and that they had no cash, officials discussed the wildly unrealistic possibility of each Sayisi Dene family raising $1,000 cash for a down payment and receiving a $9,000 loan under the National Housing Act. At first, they were considering temporary housing because they didn't want to encourage "the Indians" to stay in Churchill. Then they talked about housing comparable to Akudlik, the community that the government had set up for the Inuit. Then they began to negotiate with the provincial government to select a piece of land. The Department of Indian Affairs was confronted with one obstacle after another. The provincial government was reluctant to sell any crown lands to the Department of Indian Affairs for housing the Dene. The director of the Manitoba Lands Branch was of the opinion that the "Indians be separated from white families."[8] Provincial authorities made progress extremely difficult. In July 1957, an Indian Affairs official wrote to R.D. Ragan: "In brief the Indians through no fault of their own, appear to be getting the run-around."[9]

By the fall of 1957, the Department of Indian Affairs had tentatively selected a site between the Roman Catholic and the Protestant cemeteries and the water pipeline. The land had earlier been the site of an army tent camp, called Camp-10. Indian Affairs now planned to erect seventeen tiny pre-fabricated cabins to house only the families who had been evicted. But, over the next two years, Camp-10 became a settlement for all the Sayisi Dene who had been displaced from their hunting and trapping grounds.

CAMP-10

A couple of kilometres from the eastern limits of the town of Churchill, a rocky, windswept patch of land rose towards the southern shore of Hudson Bay. On it, a wire fence surrounded rows of wooden crosses. This was the Churchill cemetery — a grim place, unsheltered by trees or buildings. Only stubby willow bushes and brambles grew between the black boulders scattered on the ground. There was nothing else between the rows of crosses and the enormous sky brooding over them. One of the crosses, bearing a white limestone statue of Jesus, dominated the skyline. Limestone statues of the Virgin Mary, Mary Magdalene, and Salome, the mother of two of Christ's apostles, stood in perpetual grief at its foot. Around them, the vast, empty land and the steely ocean stretched as far as the eye can see.

This was the patch of land on which the Government of Manitoba finally agreed to let the Department of Indian Affairs build a series of inexpensive[1] pre-fabricated cabins for the Sayisi Dene. In early 1958, when the first cabins went up, they were meant to provide shelter for only the fourteen families being evicted from the Harbours Board land. But, by 1959, Indian Affairs had decided to house all the Sayisi Dene in the region in the same settlement.

During the Second World War, the area had been earmarked for the military as Camp-10. Now, it was to become a model settlement, but its rows of pre-fabricated cabins made of plywood, without sewer or water, built so close together that they almost touched each other, was anything but a model. The lower part of Camp-10 (called Lower Camp) had four rows of cabins, each about six by seven metres, and each with two or three tiny bedrooms; these accommodated the large families. Upper Camp-10 rested on the crest of the hill and had two rows of one-bedroom cabins,[2] each about 3.5 by 4.5 metres, perpendicular to the rows in Lower Camp; these were reserved for older, childless couples or young, new families. A large stretch of empty land to the west separated Camp-10 from the town of Church-ill. To the east, the wire fence stretched between the houses and the cemetery. Just under 300 metres to the north lay the shores of Hudson Bay.

In the spring of 1959, the Sayisi Dene who had been relocated to North River began to move to their new location. People who had always lived scattered in the interior were now squeezed between the North Atlantic Ocean and the Churchill cemetery. By December 21, 1959, the Indian Affairs official in Churchill reported that six of the thirteen families who were moved from Duck Lake were living in Camp-10. The houses were flimsy and draughty. The hillside was open to the wind blowing from Hudson Bay. The residents had no reliable fuel supply. In winter, once a month, the Department of Indian Affairs dumped some coal on the road. People had to fight over it — but, even if they managed to take some home, they found it difficult to make a fire without kindling.

Winters were severe. Even when it wasn't snowing, the north wind rising from Hudson Bay blew snow over the hillside, submerging the settlement. Some days, people couldn't open their doors because the snowbanks would cover the houses, all the way over the rooftops. When that happened, a Churchill town employee with a snowblower would carve a high corridor on the main road that ran through the community, but the houses remained under snow.

Camp-10 had no source of fresh water. Sometimes, in winter, people melted the snow. In spring and summer, rain or melted snow collected in holes in the ground. Children played in those holes. The Department of Indian Affairs in-stalled two spigots in the settlement, providing water from the Churchill water supply, but most of the time they didn't work because the pipes seldom had enough pressure. From time to time a truck would bring water to fill barrels in the houses. Another truck collected the garbage from time to time. But trucks had difficulty getting to Camp-10 after a heavy snowfall. Broken glass and refuse were scattered on the ground between the houses, and the children played among the debris.

On that barren slope beside the cemetery, dread gripped the residents of Camp-10. Their keen survival skills, learned over centuries, were now useless. In 1960, the federal government passed a law making it legal for "Indians" to buy alcohol. This law had devastating effects on the Sayisi Dene. As anthropologist and archaeologist Virginia Petch summed up: "You move into an area where your house is on skids, you're facing the crosses of the cemetery and you've got the North wind blowing off the Bay. You've got the polar bears marching by your house. You have nothing to do. Your kids are cold, they don't have enough to eat. They're being teased and beaten up at school. Your women are being raped. Just at that time, alcohol is legalized. Just in time to destroy a people."[3]

EVA ANDERSON

Houses were built in Camp-10 for the people. It was very disturbing to our people because we were now to live a few steps away from a mass burial grounds [the Churchill cemetery]. If our people were in charge and if someone had listened to our voices, a different site may have been selected instead of next to a graveyard. Our people the Sayisi Dene had always respected the spirits of the dead. A burial ground is a sacred place, not to be disturbed, it's a resting place for our relatives who are gone to the spirit world. The white people (Indian Affairs, the government people), who made the decisions for our people, did not acknowledge our culture and traditions. Everything about our ways as a people was overlooked right from the beginning. This is why they placed us right in the middle of a burial ground to live for the next decade.

Right at the beginning, our people wanted to continue to live like we had always done, but the white people came and started bossing us around and making decisions without asking us. They made all the moves to relocate our people, they made a mess and left us like that. This is how it all started. It was wrong for them to do this to our people, we have suffered and are still suffering from the consequences of this mistake. Look at our people and our community today, the results of the hardships are still here.

ILA BUSSIDOR

I remember the day we moved from a tent on DOT Hill to a house in Camp-10. I must have been almost five years old. It was in the fall, there was already snow on the ground. That day, my parents were packing all day, wrapping our things in bundles. Later in the afternoon a white man came in a pickup truck to take us to Camp-10. He must have been from the Department of Indian Affairs.

The house smelt of paint and of new wood. It had three little bedrooms, no running water, and no washroom. Inside, there was a stove, a couch, beds, a table and chairs, the stuff Indian Affairs had put in there. In the back, it had a little plywood porch with a slop pail. After living in a tent, I thought it was huge. We didn't have many belongings but in the tent we had been crowded.

I stood at the door and looked at these rows of white houses, I think there were four rows, all identical. I remember a feeling of starting a new life as if we were becoming new people, different people. I thought we would now be white people or something like that.

I remember evenings in that new house, when we would sit around the table and my dad would tell us stories in Dene. He would pause to smoke every once in a while. Puffs of smoke would rise above his head of white hair, and float in the air. His stories were often about the Bible and about how good and evil would be judged at the end of the world. They scared me. I imagined a big cauldron of fire falling from the sky, with red-hot coals I would burn in, if I wasn't good.

My mom would be sitting there, her hair tied back in a bun, sewing. She sewed dresses and jackets for us. She always wore colourful dresses. With calm, steady movements, she would sweep and mop the floor in that house. She kept it clean. For the laundry, she had a washtub with a washboard. She wrung each piece by hand. She hung the clothes to dry above the stove or on a clothesline outside.

When you looked towards the east from Camp-10, the first thing you saw was a big white cross with a white Jesus on it. I remember my mom telling us not to go near it. For our people, burial grounds had been sacred resting places for those who had gone to the spirit world. All of a sudden, a foot away from our house was a huge cemetery where hundreds of people were buried. Once the people began to live there, the curse was on.

A few people continued to make the thirty-five-, forty-mile trip back to North River with dog-teams, to hunt. My dad was one of them. Sometimes he would bring home some caribou meat that my mom would dry for us. Many people kept their dogs even after they had lived in Camp-10 for a while. At first they continued to use the dogs to do a little bit of trapping and a little bit of hunting, but after a while they lost track of that. Little by little, they gave up. Hungry and scrawny dogs just ran loose after that.

Most of our people were in Churchill by that time, but my grandparents on my father's side, Joe and Jessie Bighead, stayed on the land at North River by themselves. The land was their life, they wouldn't leave it. In summer they would tent across from Churchill, on the west side of the Churchill River, so they could fish. They were kind and gentle people. They used to come to Churchill to visit my parents and take me back to stay with them for about a month.

I remember they always brought something for us kids — something like chocolate bars or candy. They would stay for two or three days to visit with my mom and dad, and then they would be ready to head back onto the land. When they were preparing to leave, I would sneak away. I didn't want to go with them because across the river there were no kids there for me to play with.

They would wait for me all day while someone looked for me. In the end they found me — I always got caught. My grandpa would laugh at me, and take my hand.

Even though I was always reluctant to go across the river with them, I have such good memories of the time I spent there. My grandpa and I would walk way up the rocks to get a pail of water. I remember how my grandparents used to put out a fishing net. We would wait for the tide to go out and then we would walk out into the muddy sand to see what was caught. Sometimes it was around midnight when we went out to check the net. I remember how the sand oozed around my feet as I held my grandpa's hand and walked out towards the bay in the moonlight. The next day, my granny would be outside in a teepee, cutting up all the whitefish, to smoke and dry it. I used to help her gut the fish. It would be a hot day and there would be flies buzzing around as we sat together.

After moving to Camp-10, I started grade one. The kids were swearing in a language I had never heard before. "Fuck you. Fuck off." Things like that. I spoke some English because I had been in hospital for six or seven months and I had learned English there. But I didn't understand those words.

My mother never drank when we first moved to Camp-10. For a long time she didn't drink even after everyone around her began to drink heavily. I remember how she used to dress at that time. In the traditional Sayisi Dene way, she'd wear a dress, bright socks, and shoes. Her quarter-length jacket had a gathering around the waist. She always wore a colourful scarf.

At bedtime, my mom made us kneel down and say the Lord's Prayer in Dene, every night. To this day I remember the first line of the Lord's Prayer in Dene: "Nu'tha ya k'ai the da." Then she would tuck us in, give us a goodnight kiss, and tell us to be quiet because if we laughed or made noise e'thzil (night spirits; the spirits of the dead) would hear us. The house was warm, silent.

I think it was the first winter at Camp-10 that my sister Caroline got married. Her wedding in that house in Camp-10 was the very first wedding I saw in my life. Caroline had a beautiful wedding gown. My granny's sons, Jimmy and Johnny Anderson, were playing the guitar and the fiddle. The people were square-dancing. We were standing on the counter so we could see over the tops of people's heads. The house was packed like a sardine can. I also remember a woman named Celia Jawbone who was there with an Inuit guy. They were kissing and we were spying on them and laughing. All of a sudden, the door flew open and a gust of wind blew in, and boisterous man came dancing in like a ball rolling in.

I remember my mom putting us in a room and staying there with us. My mom was looking after three young children in those days. She was raising my sister Caroline's older daughter as well as my little sister Marjorie and me. She was very protective of us kids. When people were drinking, she would keep me, my little sister Marjorie, and my niece all in a bedroom so nobody would fall on us or hurt us if a fight broke out.

We used to walk to school and back. It was a long walk. In winter we walked through deep snow. The wind was so sharp it would cut my breath. Between Camp-10 and the townsite there was nothing to give us shelter. No trees, no buildings. You couldn't even see the sky from the blowing snow.

The snow was so high that some days we couldn't open the door until somebody came and opened it from the outside. Mountains of snow would rise around the house halfway up the windows. We used to dive into the snow from the roof of our house.

From Camp-10, we would walk to St. Paul's Anglican Church in town to attend midnight mass on Christmas Eve. A long walk. At the church, after mass, they'd give us some candy and oranges. I think that's the only time anyone gave us presents. Then we would walk back.

In summer there were always puddles on the ground; the frozen land didn't absorb the water. Mosquitoes and black flies would buzz around in clouds. We sometimes climbed on the rocks behind the houses, looking for berries. The rocks were covered with moss. There were purple and yellow flowers among the weeds. People picked wild blackberries and blueberries.

I remember going swimming down at the bay, skipping down the cliffs to the shore while huge waves came crashing in. We jumped from rock to rock over deep puddles and wrote our names and drew pictures with chalk on the flat surfaces of big gray rocks.

In Camp-10, people used to put rocks together to make a campfire so they could cook meat or bannock, and make tea, outside. On summer days, they made make-shift teepees with sticks and old blankets for shade and sat around in front of the houses.

I remember a Treaty Day when there was a drum dance. We were all excited when there was a drum dance. People would gather outside. The dancers would be holding their cigarettes in their hands, and we kids would grab those cigarettes. I remember how much I loved the drum music, as if that beat awakened all that was free and strong in me. It was something I knew.

My dad was drinking already when we moved to Camp-10. After a while, I began to see a lot of drunk people. People say it was the early sixties when everyone started to drink heavily.

There was an old man named Sandy Ellis. When he was drunk in the middle of the night, he would begin to sing this beautiful song. My dad sang too when he was drunk. It was eerie. Their spirits were calling for their lost way of life.

I was still a little kid when there was a house fire at Camp-10 and some kids died. We were standing out there, the house burnt in front of our eyes with three or four kids trapped inside. The summer after that fire, they put a new floor on that foundation and there was a fiddle dance. There were lots of people there and a lot of people were drinking. I remember wondering why they were dancing on top of a house that had burnt with kids in it.

The army base in Churchill was a bustling place with apartments, a hospital, a movie theatre, a bank, a radio station, and a store. We called it Camp. Lots of kids would walk to the movies there. I remember a whole bunch of us running around in the hallways of those barracks, bumming money from people, sneaking into the shows, crawling around on the floor picking up gum and stuff like that. We would steal comics and candy from the store and the coffee shop.

One day, when I was seven or eight years old, my little sister Marjorie and I were waiting for the bus to get back into town from Camp. From town, we would walk back to Camp-10. We met a teenage girl from Camp-10. She took us to the coffee shop and bought us Coke. But then, she asked us to steal comics for her. We did. She got on the bus with us. We were supposed to get off the bus at Hearne Street, but we didn't. This girl made us get off on another street.

It was early evening, not quite dark yet. She walked towards one of the houses down the street, where some guys were working on a car. She stopped and talked to the guys, then called us over. We all got into the car. The teenage girl got in the back with one of the guys, my little sister and I got in the front. I remember my sister didn't want to sit beside the driver so I had to sit in the middle.

The girl started necking in the back seat. We were scared. The driver was driving really slowly and the car began to go up and down, up and down. We didn't dare to look back but we knew what was going on. They were having sexual intercourse in the back seat while we sat in the front. This car was driving all over the place and not going to Camp-10. Finally, they finished doing what they were doing in the back seat. The guys drove us to Camp-10. We got out and went home.

I remember the very first time I saw someone having sex. There were a whole bunch of us little kids, about seven or eight of us, standing in somebody's house, in front of a doorway. In the room two people were having sexual intercourse. I was very young, I didn't know what was going on, I had no idea what they were doing. All of a sudden the guy saw us standing there, and he screamed at us. We just scattered and ran out of the house. After that, it became a common thing to see that. When people were drunk, they would be doing it anywhere. The houses in Camp-10 had no doors or curtains to separate the rooms anyway. There was no privacy for anyone.

Some nights I used to wake up and see a guy come in and force himself on my sister. He would rape her while I lay in the same room, seeing everything.

One spring day when I was about eight years old, I experienced for the first time the feelings of foreboding and dread that were to become a part of my life. I came home from school that day and noticed right away that the house my mom kept tidy until then was in shambles. My parents were sitting together at the table. Their eyes looked strange, as if they didn't see me. I had seen my dad drunk before. I recognized that look. But my mom! I had never seen my mom drunk in my life. Her speech was slurred. Her hair was untidy.

A desolate feeling came over me, an ache, a heaviness in my soul, a certainty that something was very wrong. After that day, every time my mom and dad would drink, that same feeling of loss, of hopelessness, of loneliness, would come over me. From then on, I lived with that feeling. I still experience it today.

After my mom started drinking, she stopped making sure we were in bed on time or making us say the Lord's Prayer before sleep. She stopped fixing our hair. We no longer had clean clothes. Our lives gradually changed because now my parents began to fight. It was as if the world was beginning to turn dark. My mom had been so careful to protect us. Now it became the other way round, we had to try to protect her.

She started to drink more and more until it became a regular thing. When my parents got drunk, they also got angry with each other. I remember running to stand between them to prevent them from hitting each other.

Sometimes we would go to bed and our parents would be arguing and shouting all night long. People would be coming in and out of the house. My little sister Marjorie and I would hang around to try to make sure that nothing bad happened to our parents. We would try to keep other drunk people away so things wouldn't get out of hand.

One night, after my mom and dad had passed out in a bedroom, two men were sitting in our living room and whispering to each other. There were some other little kids in the house with us, but when I saw those men whispering, I knew right away that they wanted to go into the room where my mom had passed out. I think they were planning to rape my mom. My little sister and I were scared but determined to protect our mom, so we stayed in that room. Those men tried to chase us out but we wouldn't go. The men finally left.

I remember how I used to come home and Mom and Dad used to be drunk, passed out. A feeling of such loneliness would come on me that I would crawl into bed with Mom. I used to hug her, feel her body heat, and tell myself she was okay, that I was there to be with her. One night, when I had gone to bed with her like that, she woke up in the middle of the night. She woke me up. "Sele" ("My daughter"), she said, "can you get me some water?" I didn't want to get up because I was sleepy. She took my hand and she placed my fingers on her tongue. Her tongue was dry like sandpaper. She was just sobering up. I got her a big dipper of water. She downed that. I went and got her another one. She was so dehydrated from drinking.

I also remember how she used to get up in the morning and look around to see what there was for a fire. I remember how cold it was in the house. It wouldn't warm up. All houses at Camp-10 were like that. They just didn't warm up.

After my mom started to drink we began to run around the graveyard in the middle of the night. We didn't know how much our parents had respected burial grounds. We used to run around there making a lot of noise and look at the names on the stones. Sometimes, we'd take flowers off somebody's grave and put them on someone else's grave. How were we to know the taboos of our tradition, when our parents and elders were already in darkness? The white statue of Jesus stared at us from that big cross.

ERNIE BUSSIDOR

I know the exact date when we moved to our new house in Camp-10: June 1, 1959, a month before my third birthday. On that day, my grandfather put a pillow on my back, he tied it with a string across my shoulders. It was my load. In fact, I carried two pillows, on two separate trips, to Camp-10.

I was being raised by my grandparents. Until then, we had been living in a shanty at the edge of town. On the day of the move, we walked along the pipeline, all the way to our new house. That pipeline that went right behind our little shanty all the way to Camp-10 was like a highway people travelled on when they were moving.

We had the key. My grandpa opened the door while a guy was standing on a stepladder, printing our house number on the wall: 2. There were minimal basic furnishings in the house. Everything was new. I was happy.

My uncle was twelve years older than me. He was into the Beatles and Bill Haley and the Comets. That music was blaring through his room.

For about a year, there was no alcohol in Camp-10. In the fall, our family and another family, the Mowatts, headed up to Herriot Creek with dog-teams. The two families tented there and fished. There was a woodstove in the tent. My grandparents and John Mowatt and his wife caught big jackfish. The Mowatts' son Tommy and I played stick hockey on the ice with a tin can. We used to walk around with snowshoes and get wood with our parents. John Mowatt was a good man. He had a beautiful wife.

Travelling with dog-teams, and fishing and hunting, disappeared gradually. Within a couple of years we began to see people drunk.

In our culture we bury the dead far away from the living, because we believe the spirits linger near burial grounds and they can make people sick. At Camp-10 we were beside the cemetery. When people started dying from alcohol, they were buried right next door. Mothers and grandmothers would be weeping and mourning in front of us. You could hear them ten feet away from you, people lying beside a grave, crying. Sometimes they would be drunk. It sent chills up people's backs. Everyone was uneasy. And those deaths! Those weren't natural losses. Those were shocking deaths. In Camp-10, gradually we became immersed in tragedy.

As a three- or four-year-old little boy, I remember I used to walk around the house crying, sleepwalking every night. I had this craving, this need that made me cry. Looking back, I realize what it was — I was looking for love. I never got love. Not from my mother, not from my grandparents, not from my uncle. Just this aching need.

Before I started school, the house next door to us burnt down. There were some children inside. Our house was right next door so we had to get out and stand outside. It burned to the ground in front of our eyes in a matter of minutes.

I think it was also around that time that I saw the body of the grandfather of the Thorassie family up in the rocks. People knew there was a missing elder in the community. One evening, a lot of people were walking around on the rocks between Camp-10 and Churchill, on the north side of the water pipeline. It was summer, but the weather was kinda cool. I remember some people began to yell.

I went running down there, and between the rocks and blackberry, redberry, beds, this old man was lying in a narrow crevice. He was in his long-johns. He had been murdered. There was alcohol involved in his death, but there were no suspects. It was a peculiar incident.

Soon I began to see a family friend drunk, beating his wife. Their son was my friend. I used to hang out with him. Sometimes we saw his mother outside, naked and bruised, while his father was passed out inside.

Slowly, something awful crept on us. It was such a gradual thing that we became accustomed to it.

SARAH CHEEKIE

I didn't know English. I went from the bush to the school. I remember my first day of school quite clearly. My brother Fred was a year ahead of me, but he was in the same room that year. There were lots of white kids. I used to think they had funny-coloured hair.

During a lesson on arithmetic, the teacher came up to me and gave me two crayons, an orange and a yellow, and a picture of a duck. She was an older woman. I had no clue what she was saying. I looked at the crayons and I thought maybe she wants me to scribble. I didn't know how to colour. It just happened that the day before, my mom and dad had taken us to the Bay and got us forty-eight colour crayons. I took those crayons and started colouring that duck in all kinds of different colours. For some reason, that woman came and she hit that desk really hard. I knew nothing about getting hit. She was also screaming away but I don't know what she was saying.

Then she grabbed that math book, she tore off that page and she gave me a new one, and she slapped down those crayons again, the orange and the yellow. I just sat there. I kind of froze because she had been screaming at me. Our parents never did that to us. She then pulled me forward, she hit the desk again and walked away.

My brother Fred was sitting in front of me. He turned around to look at me, and that woman hit him hard with a yardstick. Fred just got up and pushed that old woman and said "C'mon" to me. We got out of the classroom.

We went as far as that grain elevator at the mouth of the Churchill River. There were trains going in front of it, and we had to go inside a train to get to the other side of the tracks. The boxcars were moving. I was screaming because I was scared. Fred kept pulling me and we kept going. There's a bridge there with big holes on it. I always thought I'd fall through those holes so I didn't want to cross that bridge. It took Fred a long time to persuade me to go on it. Finally we got to the other side and got home.

Mom wasn't drinking then. She asked what happened and we told her. The next day I didn't want to go back to school. My dad took us. He was wearing a blue suit with yellow stripes. He went up to that woman and said, "Don't you ever hit my kids again. I don't hit my kids." That was my introduction to school.

Things got worse. The language was a mystery. I didn't understand English. Everything was totally different from what I had known living in the bush with my mom and dad. It was also noisy.

But during my first year at school there was this little white girl. I still remember her name: Barbara Sheboya. Her hair was all in curls, and she was the one who taught me how to speak English.

One day a whole bunch of kids were playing ball. I was just standing there because there were so many kids and they were so different from us. Barbara kept throwing that ball at me and I threw it back at her. She smiled and started talking to me. I didn't know what she was saying, but as we started getting school work, she started to teach me and I caught on real fast. She was kind. She was my friend. I went to school with her till grade five and then her parents moved away.

By the time I was in second grade, I was speaking English fluently. It's difficult to translate between English and Dene because some English words don't exist in Dene and some Dene expressions don't have an equivalent in English.

There were also Cree and Métis students at the school. They were mean to us. If we had nice clothes on, they would tear them. I had long hair that my mom used to braid carefully for school. They used to pull my hair until the braids came out. But gradually I got tough. I learned not to let anybody push me around. I fought back. I stood my ground. The Cree kids soon started recognizing it and respecting me.

My mom started drinking when I was in grade three. Until then, we were dressed cleanly. But when she drank, she couldn't get up in time to dress us. There were no more clean clothes. We used to get out of bed. No fire in the house. Everything frozen. There was no such thing as a shower. The water in the pitcher was cold with ice floating in it. There was no breakfast, no lunch. If Mom had a little money and if she did have a chance to go to the store, we might have something to eat after school. We would just get dressed and go to the bus and go to school like that. And then you're sitting in class and all those white kids are laughing at you 'cause you're dirty, your hair is not combed. That's how we went to school right through grade four.

RUBINA YASSIE

I got married in 1948, and we came to Churchill because my husband began to do casual labour in Churchill. My husband was a good hunter, a good trapper. He made a good living. We had everything we needed. When my husband earned some money for furs or for doing occasional jobs, it was I who decided how it would be spent. We spent it wisely on food and on tools we needed. I was always dressed well, and so were my husband and my kids.

After people started drinking in Churchill, I never saw money again. My husband had control over what little we were given. He spent everything on alcohol.

Everybody suffered from all kinds of abuse, but I feel that my suffering was among the worst because I had a lot of small children at that time. I had seven children, five of them under the age of eight. I tried to look out for my children, none of them froze or was injured seriously. I thank God for that.

When my husband drank, he beat me. I was in hospital twice because he beat me. I remember bitterly cold winter nights when I used to run out in the middle of the night with all my small children. In the howling wind, I would run for my life and go from house to house, to see who would let me in. I would bang on the doors until someone took pity and let me in with my children. When someone let me in, I would curl up on the bare floor and my small children would all lay their heads on my body for warmth because we had no covers, no blankets, no mattress.

When I woke up the next morning, my first thought would be, I have to go home. When I walked into my house, my husband would be there and he wouldn't say anything to me because all that happened the night before would be when he was drunk. When he was sober, he was a different man.

When my husband and I were sober, we worked together and joked and laughed together. I would sew and make mitts or slippers to sell. When I sold them in town, I would buy a case of wine with six bottles to a case. When we started drinking we would be happy and we would laugh, but as my husband got drunk, he would start abusing me.

He went to jail twice for beating me up. Both times he got five months in jail. But through all this, we never left each other.

As my children got older, they began to sleep outside. When I sobered up in the morning, I would start to look for them. They would be all sleeping under the house, on the sand. I usually looked until I found all of them. It was their way of escaping from drunken parents. It was safer for them under the houses.

So many people died in Churchill, all my brothers and my sister. My husband died there from alcohol too. He just drank himself to death one night. When he died, I continued to drink and I cried all the time. I didn't want to live. My small children would be hanging on to me. Talking about the past is hard because your heart cannot bear the pain.

Alcohol Takes Over

Unable to hunt or trap, scorned by the townsfolk of Churchill, living in grinding poverty, and filled with a sense of powerlessness and loss, most of the adults at Camp-10 became addicted to alcohol. Within a couple of years, their community collapsed into disorder and despair.

The residents of Camp-10 lived in constant fear. Camp-10 was on a polar-bear path, and the people felt exposed and defenceless. Polar bears were an endangered species, so town officials didn't allow firearms in the settlement.[1] The Sayisi Dene had believed the government would look after them. They waited. But gradually an even deeper sense of helplessness and loss descended upon them.

In 1962, the Anglican bishop expressed frustration and regret about the situation of the Sayisi Dene in Camp-10:

> Their present condition in Churchill we regard as being a most unhappy plight for a group of Indians who were accustomed to the life of hunting and trapping of the north. Their life has always been a most rigorous one, filled with hardship and the lack of many of the amenities of normal modern life. However, at Churchill, very little has been done to establish them there in the community enterprises. . . . I believe it was a grave error to move them from their trapping grounds simply to make it easier for authorities to give them the relief that obviously they now need.[2]

Living near the cemetery was deeply disturbing for the people who believed that *e'thzil* (restless spirits) would linger near burial grounds. Out of respect for spirits, they had always stayed away from graves and destroyed the belongings of dead people. During their years of hunting and trapping, whenever someone died at a campsite, they would move away. Now, they had no choice but to live facing the graves.

In July 1963, sixteen-year-old Peter Thorassie hand-wrote a letter on behalf of Chief John Clipping to the regional director of Indian Affairs in Winnipeg, asking that the people be moved away from the cemetery to land near the river. He wrote: "The Chipewyan people do not want to live next to the dead people. Many of our people think that the dead people get up at twelve o'clock midnight and walk around our camp for half an hour. The younger people do not always believe in these spirits."[3]

In 1964, Martha Commodore was relieving the public health nurse in Churchill. She remembers being horrified by the plight of the Sayisi Dene: "The first thing that bothered me was that they were living beside the cemetery. I remember hearing people wailing — weeping on the rocks. I was staying at the Hudson motel, and sound travels through the open space, so you would hear it. As I got to know the people, I realized some of the wailing would happen during a drum dance. In their sorrow, they would cry out." In 1966, seven years after the establishment of Camp-10, William Koolage, an anthropologist from the University of North Carolina, studied the community for his doctoral dissertation. In it, Koolage describes the Sayisi Dene's sense of dislocation and despair. He wrote that one man burst into tears one night, crying, "I'm lonely for the caribou. I'm lonely for Duck Lake."[4] Koolage also reports that all the Sayisi Dene adults he met became melancholy and even hysterical when the subject of Duck Lake or the caribou hunt came up. He also found that many older men and women refused to talk about the past because the Anglican priest had discouraged them from doing so.[5]

As the adults in Camp-10 became alcoholic, they could no longer care for or protect their children. Eventually, many parents were not able to provide their children with proper food. They were unfamiliar with store-bought food and didn't know how to prepare it. The natural balance of their traditional diet had been lost as soon as they arrived in Churchill. Soon they discovered they could trade food rations for cash to buy alcohol. When people received their meagre welfare vouchers from the Department of Indian Affairs, they rushed to buy expensive meats like steak, roast, or turkey. They would take that meat around town and sell it for a fraction of its worth, and then they would buy alcohol with the cash. This practice became a pattern. "If a roast is worth sixteen dollars, they would approach someone and ask, 'Can you give me two dollars for this?' With the two dollars, they would buy cheap wine. Meanwhile, there was nothing for the kids to eat at home. When the welfare was gone and the booze was gone, then it was desperation. They had no choice but to go to the garbage dump to scrounge around for food. Kids and adults were scrounging around, looking for scraps continuously, like animals" (Ila Bussidor).

Some of the most painful memories of Sayisi Dene survivors are associated with the garbage dumps in Churchill. The Sayisi Dene made regular excursions to the dump, located about five kilometres south of town, to rummage in the mounds of refuse for scraps of food, clothing, toys, or copper wire. Children scrounged around the garbage heaps behind the local hotels and bars. They looked for leftovers, cigarette stubs, scrap metal — anything they could consume or trade. Even the few families whose adults didn't drink ate food from the dump.

> I remember my grandparents used to go to the dump every Sunday. It was a community event. Everyone filed in single file almost, to the dump. (Ernie Bussidor)

> As a little girl, I used to have to go to the dump with my mom. We sometimes made a fire to warm up, and if a truck came along, we used to rush to hide behind the rocks until it went away. We used to go by the banks of Hudson Bay. There were always ravens going round and round above our heads. At that point our people didn't have much choice. They had nothing to look forward to. They just gave up hope. (Caroline Bjorklund)

Eventually, relations between the children and the adults broke down completely. Traditionally, children would have been helping with the tasks of survival — boys would be cutting firewood, girls would be bringing in water or snow to melt for washing and cooking. Now, the children were at school, losing their own language, learning English, and fending for themselves in an environment about which their parents knew nothing. The parents spoke only Dene, and soon family members could no longer communicate with each other.

When the parents drank, the children had no protection or guidance, and only each other for support. Camp-10 had no recreational activities. The Sayisi Dene children were out of place at the sports events of other groups in the town. Other children scorned them. The youngsters of Camp-10 began to hang around in packs for protection. Soon they were out of control and in trouble.

At night, they ran wild on the gravel roads of Camp-10 and in the streets of Churchill, until three or four o'clock in the morning. They threw stones at the dogs to make them howl, they broke windows of houses. They spied on the adults in the settlement and mugged drunks, or broke into houses to steal wine or food. These were their favourite games. If an adult offended a youngster, a pack of kids would take revenge by attacking and beating the adult when he or she was most vulnerable — when drunk. There were no streetlights in Camp-10. It was hard to recognize who was in the gang, who was hitting, kicking, or stabbing. Teenagers began to break into stores to steal cigarettes, liquor, candy, chips.

MARY YASSIE

During this time my parents were not involved in alcohol. They looked after us the best they could; we were always protected. When they started drinking along with the rest of the people, it's like they just forgot about us. We were no longer cared for and, instead, alcohol came first in their lives. We started to live a life that was totally different from before. We the children were infested with head lice until we became older and learned how to look after ourselves. In just about every family, ways of living changed around this time, for the worst, and the children were the ones who suffered the most, like my small brothers and sister and me. After the people started living in Camp-10 next to the graveyard, I remember many hard times when my parents were always drunk and we were forever looking for a safe place to sleep. This one night when my parents were drunk and fighting, I went with my friend to sleep with her at her grandmother's place. They didn't have enough blankets, and we made a bed on the floor with jackets, I went to bed on the floor. This was during the winter and I just about froze, I'll always remember this. The houses that were built for the people were not warm enough. They weren't fit to live in.

I went to school in Churchill along with the rest of the kids from Camp-10, and the abuse we went through in the school is something I'll never forget. As soon as they knew we were Dene kids from Camp-10, they would start picking on us, calling us names, pulling our hair. This type of treatment went on all through the year, and yet the teachers never paid any attention to what was going on. When I became a teenager I didn't like what was happening to my family. There was nothing but drinking going on at home, there was never food for the kids, just people drunk and fighting. I started hanging out with a group of teenagers who started to rebel against what was taking place in Camp-10 and the prejudice from the town people against the Dene. We started to drink and get into all sorts of trouble around town. We started to break into stores and steal whatever we could take — food, clothing, jewellery, and liquor — anything we could get our hands on. I was only about thirteen years old during this time. I was thrown in jail along with the other kids after we were caught breaking into the hotel and the liquor store, just to steal booze. Since my parents were already heavy into the drinking, it seemed like they didn't care that I was doing these things, they didn't see that I was suffering just like they were.

ILA BUSSIDOR

I have a memory from when I was ten years old. It was a spring day, and much of the snow had melted away. I was playing somewhere around the house. An old couple, Sarah and John Kithithee, were going to the dump. They called out to me and asked if I wanted to go with them. I got really excited because I wanted to go. They told me to go home and ask my parents. It must have been a Sunday or a Monday because my parents were sober. They said it was okay.

We were at the dump all day, collecting food (things like wieners and baloney) and anything else that was useable. This man, John Kithithee, packed everything I collected in a little box for me. He measured the distance between my shoulders and then measured the box because I was going to carry it home on my back. It was a good ten- or twelve-kilometre walk.

As we were walking, we passed the army base where all these white people lived, and I remember feeling ashamed. But I got home, and I brought this box of food with me. My mom smiled and put the box on the table. My dad was standing by the window. I saw that he was crying. "I was a proud man," he said. "I hunted, and trapped for my family. I was so proud, I never wore clothes that were even a little damaged. But today my little girl brings food home from the garbage dump so I can eat."

Just about everybody in Camp-10 used to walk to the town dump to collect scrap copper. They collected copper wire, stripped the wire of its insulation by heating it in metal pots over an open fire, then melted the copper down and pounded it and took it to two men in town named Windy Smith and Joe Cole. I remember many times when I went there with my mom and dad. My parents carried this scrap copper on their backs in a bag or a box. I remember how Joe Cole would put it on a scale and weigh it. I think he paid something like twenty-five cents a pound for that. My parents would then go downtown and buy a little bit of food, but they were doing it mostly for booze. A group of people would chip in together after buying the booze and take a cab back to Camp-10. I used to think it was fun. Now when I look back, I can understand the desperation that made people do that.

It was a common thing for kids to hang out in town till all hours of the night. All of us kids would hang around in packs while everybody was drinking. We were always in packs. We would hang around behind the Churchill Hotel and the Hudson Hotel and dig into the garbage.

At the hotel, they would throw out lots of cigarette butts, and we would collect them. We stuffed them in our pockets or found a bag and stuffed them in. We were always behind the hotels or behind the stores digging around in the garbage cans as if we were animals.

The Churchill train station was one of the places where we used to hang out. The train would be sitting there smoking and steaming while we stood on the gravel parking lot or on the platform, waiting for the tourists to come out. Trainloads of tourists came to Churchill every summer, mostly senior citizens. Before they spread throughout the town, they would take pictures of us and throw nickels and dimes at us. That's why we hung around at the station. We also checked out the station's dump because the tourists often threw food away — tons of cake, pies, things like that. We would take those things and eat them.

Those weren't the only places we scrounged around. There was also this cook house behind the barracks where the men who worked at the grain elevator stayed. It had stairs and a little door. Our people used to go there with pails, and instead of throwing things like leftover soup into the garbage can, the cooks would pour that stuff into these pails for those who were standing there. I remember going there many times with adults. Soup and sausages. That was a gold mine! A real resource. We were like ravens or vultures.

Kids and adults were scrounging around, looking for scraps continuously, like animals. No wonder the townspeople looked down on us. "Dirty garbage pickers," they called us. "You dirty Chipewyans!"

My mom had a friend named Jean. Jean was a young, beautiful woman who used to come to our house for a visit from time to time. I remember hearing Jean tell my mom how one night she had been picked up and thrown in jail for being drunk even though she hadn't been drunk. She told my mom the cops had thrown her in the back of a paddy wagon, and instead of taking her to jail, they had driven her way past the army base, way past the dump. There, they had gang-raped her. The RCMP! Then they had put her back in the paddy wagon, they had taken her back to town and thrown her in jail. She wasn't drunk but this is what happened to her. She was telling my mom all this in a manner that was almost matter-of-fact. It was as if she was resigned to her fate.

Later, Jean did drink. She was sent to the women's jail in The Pas on drinking charges, and she died there. She had three small children. When a Dene was sent to jail for drinking, many of the white people in Churchill would mock them and say that the Dene were "off on vacation."

After my mom started drinking, I began to see her getting beaten. One night, when I was about nine years old, we were sleeping on the floor in the living room. My mom was drunk. She was yelling. My dad was in another room. He too was yelling from in there. When my mom and dad drank, they didn't sleep together because they fought so much. They argued and shouted all night long.

One of my brothers came to the doorway. I guess he was fed up with the yelling. He said, "Why don't you shut your fucking mouth!" He threw a boot across the room. Those boots were called Beatle boots. They had a big heel on them, with a zipper on the side. He threw it, and hit my mom in the face. I remember my mom's lip split open with the blow. She had a big cut on her lip. Blood spurted all over the place. I was crying and looking for something to put on my mom's mouth. She never got stitches for that wound.

Other memories of people abusing my mother come back to me from time to time. They're like nightmares, almost unbearable. I remember a summer day. My mom came home from downtown with one of my sisters, who was about eight months pregnant. My sister's husband had been drinking. He started to pick a fight with her. My mom got in the way, saying, "Don't hurt her, she's pregnant." The man then turned on my mom. I saw him kicking my mom in the face and throwing her around. My mom was crying. Everybody was shouting and there was blood all over the place.

I remember a neighbour's son was there wearing a white shirt. He had this plastic pail in his hand and he was running down the road to the water tap, to get a pail of water to take to my mom.

Our neighbours called the cops in the end. The cops came and took my sister's husband away. He went to jail and did time for beating my mom. It left a scar across her upper lip that remained for the rest of her life.

Some nights when people were drinking and fighting everywhere in the ghetto, we would take refuge in the house of a little old lady. We called her *Sanquatse* (Little Old Lady). Her last name was Mowatt. She was blind. She didn't drink. Her tiny, wee house with just a stove and a bed was the only safe place where there was heat and a sober person. All these kids would crowd in there, getting warm and hiding from drunk people.

The next day, we would go home and find everybody hungover. They'd be trying to clean up and pick up the pieces of their lives. But that same day, before the evening rolled around, they were in the same situation again. And we, the kids, would be running around in the streets in all hours of the night.

A party starts. People begin to drink. They're talking to each other, being nice to each other, laughing at each other's jokes. They're getting mellow, enjoying themselves. But as the party goes on and they drink more, they gradually change. I hear them getting louder and louder, I see them spilling their drinks, their cigarette ashes fall all over the place, they knock something over. Soon, the mellowness is gone. They start to shout and yell and swear. The next thing you know, they start to argue. They shove each other. A little later, a fight breaks out. They punch each other, kick each other in the face. They no longer know what they're doing. They're completely different people from what they were an hour or two ago. The next thing you know, it's getting really ugly. Somebody is getting beaten up bad. Someone calls the cops.

The children are scared. They're hiding, peeking out from behind the doors or from under the beds. The children run out into the cold night. There's a blizzard. The snow is blowing, the wind is howling and we little kids, we're shivering, standing at the side of the house.

I close my eyes and I still see that little girl standing there, helpless, not knowing where to go, waiting for people to stop fighting or to pass out, or for the cops to get the people out of the houses. We're freezing and scared — scared of our own adults: our parents, brothers, and sisters, who are fighting. If there's a light on in somebody's house, we knock. We hope they're sober. Most of the time they're not. We always hope somebody will be kind enough to let us in and to let us sleep inside. Where do we turn but to each other for comfort and protection?

In summer, we would sleep under the houses, under the cement foundations. We had blankets in there, candles, all kinds of stuff. When the adults were drinking and fighting in the house, a whole pack of us would crawl through a hole under the house to escape. We would cover the hole with a board and put a bunch of rocks against it because we were afraid hobos would come and steal us while we slept.

There was no way to heat the houses at Camp-10, no trees people could cut to use as firewood. One man, who had eight children and who spoke a little English, went to the Indian agent and asked for fuel. The Department of Indian Affairs began to bring in a pile of black coal once a month. They would dump it outside the houses. It wouldn't catch fire without kindling, and it was never enough.

Many, many times, after a night of people drinking all night long, screaming their heads off, fighting, slamming the door going in and out of the house while we tried to sleep, we would have to get up, and the house would be freezing. People would pass out in the wee hours, Mom and Dad would pass out and quit screaming at each other, and then we would have to get up at eight o'clock in the morning.

No heat. There was no wood. It was really hard to make a fire in the morning because you can't make a fire with coal alone. You have to start looking for scraps. The water in the water tank would be frozen. You had to use an ax to break the ice. There would be ice floating in the bowl of water we washed our faces with. Sometimes, my mom would make a fire, somehow. The stove wasn't fit for that climate so it was really hard to get it going. We would be standing around the stove trying to keep warm.

Nothing to eat. My mom would heat up some water and put a little bit of canned milk in it. I remember she would add a teaspoonful of lard, stir it and say, "This won't fill you, but at least it'll help you get through the day." We would drink that and get on the school bus.

I can imagine how we must have looked. We didn't sleep in pyjamas and stuff like that. We just jumped into bed the way we were dressed after running around all hours of the night. In the morning, we wouldn't even change our clothes or wash our hair or anything like that. We'd go to school like that. No wonder other kids scorned us.

I was going to school in town with the white, Cree, and Inuit kids. They all had these neat lunches packed with them. I remember standing there and watching them at lunch time. Most of the time we didn't have lunch. I was hungry. I remember one occasion when a girl was unpacking an apple, a banana, and a Coffee Crisp bar. I couldn't take my eyes off that candy bar. The girl watched me too. I'd be standing there, feeling hungry, envious, and ashamed. Ashamed that I was Dene because it meant where I came from there was nothing but drunk people and there was no food.

Sometimes my mom would put some sweetened tea into a peanut butter jar or a jam jar. We used to call that sugar juice. She would tear the plastic from a bread bag and cover that jar and screw the top on it so it wouldn't spill, and she would put it in a bag for us to take to school. Other kids would make fun of us because we had these jars full of tea.

There were times when we stayed up all night and didn't go to school the next day because our parents were hungover or they were still drunk. The truant officer would come to Camp-10. He would pile us into a car and take us to school in town. And one by one, we would all get strapped.

I remember how we would line up in the principal's office, like a herd of cattle, all these Dene kids, filthy dirty. Our names would be called one at a time, we would go into the principal's office. He would pull our pants down and strap us on the bum with a big leather strap. I remember being strapped like that many times, on my bare bum. You ask anyone my age, any Dene kid of my generation, and they'll tell you each and every one of them have had strappings. They didn't do that to the other kids, white or Métis, or Cree or Inuit. It was the Dene kids who got the strap.

One time, the truant officer collected a bunch of us from attics, from under the houses. He dragged us from under the houses, from under the beds, from wherever we were hiding, literally dragged us and took us to school. There were twelve or fifteen of us. We hadn't washed up, and we must have looked terrible. One by one, we were called to get a strapping. I was so scared, I stood there shaking. My time was coming. You could hear each kid who went into that office screaming and crying in pain. Everyone came out humiliated. I stood there, terrified. I was the next in line. They called my name.

The principal's name was Mr. Jahns, and the truant officer was Mr. Wiebe. The kids from Camp-10 despised them. They asked, "Are you Ila Cheekie?" I said, "Yes." I guess I hadn't said yes loudly enough, because the principal shouted, "What?" "Yes," I said. Then, he asked me the strangest thing. "Are you a woman?" he asked. I didn't know what he was saying. What I thought he meant was, "Are you a boy or a girl?" I said, "Yes," shaking more than ever. Then, he said, "You can leave." He didn't strap me. I went out of the room.

Years later, I understood what he meant. When he said "Are you a woman?" he was asking "Do you have your period?" I didn't have my period, but I saved myself because I thought he was asking if I was a boy or a girl. Isn't that sad? Maybe just before I went in, he had strapped a girl who had her period.

It didn't end with the principal and some teachers. Other kids, especially the Cree, also picked on us. I remember one day three or four of us Dene girls were going to the washroom. I was about the third one to go into a stall. I sat down on the toilet, but these Cree girls were reaching over the door of the cubicle, trying to grab somebody's hair. One of them managed to grab my hair, and she threw herself to the other side so her weight was on the other side, and as she did that, she pulled me up by both hands. I was screaming and crying. My pants got all wet. I was embarrassed and humiliated. I didn't want to come out of the washroom. I was standing there, crying. One of the Dene girls went to tell the teacher. The teacher was a young, pretty woman named Mrs. Cribbs. I remember how she tried to comfort me. I didn't want her to touch me because my pants were wet and my hair was all messy.

Finally, Mrs. Cribbs talked me into coming out and she took me into the principal's office. There must have been clothes around there, because she gave me some clothes to change into.

It was a common thing for Dene kids to be abused like that in the Churchill school. The whole town of Churchill despised our people because they drank so much and because the kids ran around all over the place, breaking in, and because people would walk to the garbage dump to pick food to eat because there was no other way.

What's amazing is that some white children were kind to us. I remember a little girl who became my friend when I was in grade three. A pretty little girl with brown hair. Her name was Valerie, she was in my class. I don't remember her last name but I'll never forget that first name, Valerie. I don't even know how we became friends when all the other kids made fun of us Dene kids.

Valerie used to invite me to her house, I even remember exactly where her house used to be. But I was scared to go there. I felt dirty going into a white person's home. I remember her mother was really kind to me too. She must have seen how afraid I was when I came into their house because she used to be so gentle with me. She'd try to make me feel part of something that I couldn't be. I would stay for a while, play there a little, then I would go home.

Once, Valerie gave me some clothes. There was a purple dress in there, a satin dress with white lace frills. I wore it to go downtown to the St. Paul's Anglican Church for a Christmas concert. I was proud that I had something nice to wear. But then, I ran into some Cree girls. I heard them laughing and saying, "You look like an old granny." I suddenly felt ashamed. When I wore that same dress to school one day, Valerie said, "Oh, that dress fits you. You look nice."

I remember one winter when my oldest sister was in the women's jail in The Pas for drinking. My mom was looking after her three kids. At Christmas time, the youngest of those kids, a little two-month-old baby named Robert, got sick. Next door, there was a Christmas party with a lot of drinking and noise. One of the guys who was at that party came into our house with his wife. He stood near the door, saw the baby and he said, "It's pneumonia." I had never heard that word before. It stayed with me.

One of my sisters called a cab and took the baby to the hospital at the army camp. A couple of hours later, she returned with the baby. The doctors and nurses had taken a look at the baby and said there was nothing wrong with him. We could see he was really sick. My mom stayed up nursing him through the night. The next day was Christmas Eve. They took the baby back to the hospital. As it turned out, he did have pneumonia, and he died. They had to contact my sister in jail. I remember how she came home dressed in clean clothes. She had a brown paper bag in her hand. I remember her crying and my mom comforting her.

I started drinking in Camp-10 when I was about seven or eight. On Treaty Days when people got drunk, we stole their booze and drank it. We thought it was fun. I remember teenagers running around in packs, breaking in and stealing cases and cases of beer. They would haul those cases to the top of a rock and get drunk or they would give the booze away. It was their way of surviving what was going on around them.

When I was very little, my friends and I used to wait for these older kids to come back with their loot: candy and cigarettes and everything else. One night, my friend and I stayed up all night waiting for these kids. When they returned, we must have eaten all kinds of stuff. Things like chocolate bars, chips, and Coke. There was a little rock beside my friend's grandfather's house. We were sitting on this rock, and we had fallen asleep there, our heads on each other's shoulders. My friend's dad found us asleep like that. Before he woke us up, he went to my house, just across the street, he got my mom and dad and said, "Look at these two kids, sleeping."

One night, those teenagers broke into a pawn shop. My sister Sarah was one of them. She had hit the glass with her fist and cut her hand. She just about died, she would have bled to death. The way they were caught was that the cops followed the trail of blood all the way to our house.

I remember the cops coming in the morning. If they had come in a little later, Sarah would have been dead. She was bleeding, she was white and weak. An ambulance came, they took her to the hospital, and they saved her life. After that, she was sent away to residential school.

ERNIE BUSSIDOR

From Camp-10, it was about ten kilometres to the dump along the rocks on the shore, but my grandparents were getting old, the walk was too hard for them. I remember sometimes they would save money to take the bus to the last barracks of the army base, to K Row, right at the end of Fort Churchill. The road carried on around the corner for about three miles to the dump.

There were many times when my school friends would be on the bus and I would be getting off the bus at K Row. I used to feel humiliated getting off there, at the edge of town, to go to the dump with my grandparents while my classmates sat in the bus.

The adults seemed to know how to prepare food from the dump. They would clean it, rinse it out. But sometimes a bunch of us kids would go by ourselves. I don't know of anyone who got sick, but I'm sure we must have eaten some bad food. We must have had strong stomachs.

One Sunday, my grandparents returned home with a bag of clothes. There was a pair of pants in there that looked about my size. I tried them on. The legs were kinda short but otherwise they fit me. I was a skinny, scrawny kinda guy. So, I put on this pair of pants and this shirt and I wore them to school the next day. One of my white classmates, John, recognized those clothes. They were his. He was respectful to me, he didn't tease me. He pulled me off to the side during recess. "Ernie, where did you get those pants?"

"My grandmother found them," I said. I didn't say they were from the dump because it was always embarrassing to tell people that you actually ate and dressed from the dump.

"My mom threw those clothes away last week," John mumbled. Then he said, "Ernie, you can come home with me after school. I've got some other clothes that I don't wear that you can have." He was shorter than me, this guy, but he was skinny like me.

After school that day, I walked with him to his house on Wales Avenue. When I walked into the vestibule of his house, I froze in terror. The smell of the place was unfamiliar. The house was so clean, it was like a totally foreign world that I couldn't walk into. I was overcome with terror — it was overwhelming. I just stood by the door. I wouldn't go beyond the threshold. John asked me to come into his room with him. God forbid! I couldn't step beyond the doorway.

While I stood there in confusion, John spoke to his mom who was really nice to me. They brought me this bag of clothes. I took it and walked out the door. I kinda bolted out of there. For some strange reason, I felt unbelievably humiliated. At that time, I accepted the fact that we went to the dump. It was one thing to find something there and put it on, but somebody's charity was crushing. I never wore any of those clothes John had given me that day.

My grandparents stayed sober until 1965. My grandfather began to drink first. Then my grandmother also started. Grandpa would crack a lot of jokes with the guys. The guys would bring him alcohol so he could get going and tell funny stories. They would be rolling around the floor, laughing. But by the time they left, my grandpa would be drunk, and he and my grandma would start fighting.

Things in Camp-10 started to take a bad twist after 1963. The drinking increased. There were a lot of gang rapes. As young kids, we were witnesses to such things. It happened right in my home while my grandparents were sitting there, sober, and my brother and I were in the next room. There was a party going on, a lot of yelling and commotion. The adolescents were having their fun, raping a girl who was drunk. There was nothing my grandparents could do about it.

By then, my uncle was living with a woman. He began to drink heavily and to abuse her. He also started to abuse my grandparents and me. It seemed like he had so much anger. He would work for a month in a certain place, and he would get fired because of alcohol. The more he was in and out of jobs, the more he became angry.

I was his scapegoat in the house. He beat me. He threw me across the room by the hair. He kicked me. There was no one to protect me because my grandparents were also being abused by him. He beat them to a pulp.

I spent many nights sleeping outside. I would try to make sure things were quiet before I would go in, because if my uncle Sammy was drunk, even if he saw me outside on the road, all he had to do was to open the window and beckon to me. I would have no choice but to go in, and he would beat me. He really didn't know what he was doing because he would be blacked out when he was doing this. The next day, when he sobered up, he would be really nice to me.

The other Dene boys and I used to escape to the army base, which we called Camp. There was something like a mile and a half of corridors in there, a huge tunnel. It was our favourite place. We used to run up and down those corridors and hallways. For the first few years, the people tolerated us, but it got to a point where everyone started to look upon us as pests.

We didn't realize it at the time, but we were very destructive. We destroyed a lot of walls. We would sleep inside mattress rooms in the dormitories. We had even started getting under the hallways into the water system, into the pipes and the crawl spaces. Once you got into that system, you could get into any dormitory — you could get into any building because all the water pipes led to the dormitories. We used to find our way into canteens and we'd break into them through the underground tunnels. We were like rats living in the sewer system. That was our haven because it was always warm.

While all this was going on, I started drinking. I was six years old.

SARAH CHEEKIE

By the time I was about eleven, in grade five, we no longer spoke Dene with our parents. That's when things really started to change for me. I started getting into trouble, breaking into stores to get food, clothes. Everything went downhill.

My mom tried to take care of us. No matter how much she was under the influence of alcohol, she tried to make sure we were home safely, even at three o'clock in the morning. But we would sneak out again after she thought we were home. Our parents loved us. They would say, "Don't do this. Don't do that." But I was already out of control. I used to break in, go to court, get remanded, do the same thing the following night. My mom used to be ashamed of what we were doing, but she couldn't put a stop to it. She was heart-broken about so many things. Both my brother Fred and I started going in and out of jail.

I started getting into liquor at about thirteen. That's when another era started for me. I began to get into a lot of trouble.

One night in the fall, about eight of us broke into a garage looking for tools. One of the boys found a big bottle of Teacher's scotch. We got into that. Around midnight, we went across the street to a pawn shop. I thought I had a rock in my hand. I remember hitting that window. I guess I didn't have a rock. There was blood all over the place — I still have a big scar here. We took a lot of jewellery and money and we all scattered in different directions. I held my hand against my chest and ran towards Camp-10.

I got home, sticky all over with blood. I was pretty drunk, and out of breath from running. I put my hand under my other arm. There was no electricity in the house, so it was dark. My mom opened the door holding a little lamp. "What the hell are you doing out this late?" she said. "Get to bed." So I did. I was falling asleep, but I felt something heavy on me, all the necklaces, watches, rings, and money from the pawn store were on me.

I got up, went up to the stove. I took off some of that jewellery and stuffed it in the ashes in the bottom of the stove. Then I snuck outside and hid the rest of the stuff under a big rock, and went back in and went to bed. I knew I was in a lot of trouble, but I was scared to tell Mom. I thought I'd tell her in the morning. Meantime, I was bleeding. I passed out. I guess I had been bleeding all night.

In the morning I wanted to say "Mom" but my voice didn't come out. I was wishing she would look my way. I remember she was preparing bannock dough. A friend of my mother's came in. She was also looking for her children. She said to my mom, "I think these kids did something really bad again last night. There are candy wrappers, cigarettes, all over the place on the road."

As she was talking she looked my way. "Look at your daughter! What's that blood?" My mom ran to the bed and threw that blanket off. She started screaming; the blanket was soaked in blood. I was trying to tell her I broke into that shop but I had no voice. That's all I remember. I kinda faded in and out as they were screaming around me. The police must have arrived soon after.

The next thing I knew, I was in Winnipeg at the hospital. There was security all around me. I had just about died. They had given me a blood transfusion.

From there, they sent me to a residential reform school in Birtle. My life had to change again. They had a hard time disciplining me. I didn't want to go by their rules. That first year at residential school was one of the saddest times in my life. I was so lonely. We were forbidden from speaking our language even though there were about five girls there from Dene Village. They separated us. We weren't allowed to go home at Christmas. We had to stay there for ten months.

BETSY ANDERSON

I will tell you about the time when your two uncles, Johnny and Jimmy Anderson, my sons in their early twenties, drowned in the Churchill River.

It was a summer evening in 1963, three years after it became legal for our people to drink alcohol. I never drank because I didn't want to set a bad example for my sons, I knew it was a bad thing for us. When people poured a cup of wine for me, I used to spill it behind their backs.

Most of our people had moved to Camp-10, but we lived across the Churchill River. Your uncles were both married, they had houses in Camp-10, and they used to boat all the time. Sometimes they went whaling or fishing. They used to take the boat from our side of the river to the mainland. "Don't go across on the boat," I used to tell them. "It's too windy." I felt something would go wrong. It's amazing how a person can sense these things.

One afternoon just before darkness fell, they were going to go across the river on the boat, and they had been drinking. I went to the shore and grabbed the sides of the boat to prevent them from going. Your uncle Jimmy joked, "Don't hang on to the boat or I'll paddle your hand," so I had to let go. I watched as they headed across the river.

I had been sewing all that day. After they set out on the boat, I went back to my sewing. There were sounds coming from the river — from people whaling on boats. You could hear people talking. Your grandfather said, "They're drunk." I was worried. I hung up the jacket I was sewing and went out to stand outside the house and listen. Your grandfather said, "I think they made it safely to shore across the river." Then he went out to set the fish net.

The tide had gone out. I made myself a cigarette and lay down to rest. Just then, I heard someone crying out on the water. Your grandfather returned from setting the net. He said he had heard someone calling. We looked at each other. We knew we were helpless. We couldn't do anything because the tide had gone out. "They are drowning," he said. Even the dogs that were tied outside seemed to know what had happened. They had heard the cries too. They started to yelp in the night. It was very eerie.

There was only one other couple who lived on the east bank of the river: Joe and Jessie Bighead. Joe's boat was lying on the shore. The tide was way out, but the water was coming in just a little. We grabbed the boat and started to carry it towards the tide. Your grandfather got in it and began to row towards the direction from which we had heard the cries. Just then we heard another cry for help: "Come over here to the boat, this way!" Your grandfather was rowing as fast as he could, but suddenly darkness fell. The sky and the water became almost black.

Jessie and I went to her house. We lit the kerosene lamp and sat quietly, waiting. Some time later, we heard a boat approaching. It was your grandfather. "We found the boat, but they are gone," he said. "There's no hope of finding them alive." I went into shock, knowing that my sons were dead.

Our sons had died. All I prayed for was this: "This body of water is big, they might not find the bodies. Let us recover them and lay them to rest in the ground so at least I can see their crosses."

We didn't sleep that night. When the tide came in, we took the boat and started to row across the river. When we reached the other side, we walked to the RCMP station to tell them about the accident.

The tide was still in when they found their bodies. My son Jimmy had taken most of his clothes off. Some of the young guys on the other boats later said he had tried to save himself and his brother, but he couldn't because he was drunk. His older brother Johnny was fully dressed. Even his shoes were still on.

They took the bodies to the army hospital. I remember a corridor where people dressed in white stood in a row. We walked into a cold room to see our sons for the last time.

After that I began to drink. I drank whenever I could, as much as I could. I used to wander off by myself, crying. I can't even tell you how life was in Churchill — drinking was all there was.

DENE VILLAGE

$\int$ egregated from the town but exposed to view, Camp-10 had become an open wound on the rocky hillside beside the town cemetery. By the mid-sixties, several house fires had killed a number of adults and children. Tuberculosis was rampant, many children were being sent to hospitals in southern Manitoba for treatment, and a disproportionate number of Dene children were in foster homes.[1] Dene adults were regularly being thrown into the over-crowded Churchill jail. The misery of the Dene was on constant display, and it embarrassed town officials and federal and provincial politicians.

In 1963, Chief Clipping had expressed his people's wish to be moved to another location, "near the river," to be specific. In 1964, the *Winnipeg Tribune* ran a series of articles about Aboriginal life in Churchill, painting a grim picture. By 1966, Indian Affairs officials were beginning to make plans to move the Sayisi Dene yet again. And, yet again, they moved the people without adequate communication or preparation.

In 1966, officials decided to build a new village to house the Sayisi Dene, but selecting a suitable place became a problem. Negotiating with the provincial government proved difficult once again. Pressure was mounting from the Churchill townsfolk, politicians, and the Sayisi Dene themselves, who desperately wanted to get out of Camp-10.

In the fall of 1966, federal Assistant Deputy Minister of Indian Affairs R.F. Battle visited Churchill. At a meeting with Battle, Chief John Clipping expressed the eagerness of his people to get out of Camp-10. Department records show that Chief Clipping wanted to move because they would be farther away from town and they would have better control of the children's behaviour and of the band as a whole.[2]

After his trip to Churchill, Battle wrote to the minister of Indian Affairs: "Camp-10 is a disgrace that must be removed immediately."[3] The decision to vacate Camp-10 had already been made. Battle's pronouncement just increased the time pressure.

Indian Affairs officials chose a site away from the town, about five kilometres southeast of Churchill, past the army and navy bases, and past the Inuit community, Akudlik. The new site was on muskeg that never drained, but it did have some trees. Everyone — government officials, townsfolk, and the Sayisi Dene — believed the move would improve people's lives.

The plans didn't look bad: a townsite resembling a southern suburb, with houses on both sides of a curving gravel road winding through black spruce. The design even included running water and a sewage system — to be installed at a later date. Each house would be placed on a gravel pad and concrete raisers to prevent the heat from the house from melting the permafrost. The settlement came to be called Dene Village.

Dene Village would be made up of a combination of new houses and some old ones that were to be moved from Camp-10. The new houses were cheap copies of southern, suburban ones. They had picture windows, two entrances, and even porcelain toilets. Families began to move into them in the fall of 1967.

But the spiritual and social decay that had begun in Camp-10 moved with them to Dene Village. Once more, the houses were placed close to each other, and the large, curtainless windows allowed no privacy. Phil Dickman, a community development worker who spent several years at Dene Village, concluded that the community was designed in a way that increased the tensions between people:

Putting the houses close together has severely aggravated the adjustment problems of people who were accustomed to living out of sight of one another. As a result of the social breakdown that has taken place, close proximity of the houses to one another has increased the degradation carried out by angry and frequently drunken people against each other. There are many contributing factors for this abnormal behaviour but a primary one is a deep seated frustration at their seemingly hopeless plight.[4]

Within weeks, the houses began to look dilapidated. Picture windows, a luxury in southern suburbs, proved to be a catastrophe in the sub-arctic settlement. Bored kids threw stones at them, drunk people hurled bottles. At forty or eighty dollars a smash, replacing broken windows was out of the question. People tried to fill the gaping holes with materials such as cardboard, plastic, or tin that they found at the dump.

Both entrances to each house were exposed to wind and snow. The doors were thin, uninsulated. Heating fuel was scarce. At first, people cut the trees in Dene Village, but the green wood didn't burn. Once a month in winter, the government brought in a truckload of coal, but it was not enough.

Children ran around in the sub-arctic winter wearing tattered cardigans and running shoes. They broke into the houses through attic holes beside the chimneys, they huddled under the houses, in the spaces between the concrete foundation and the floor.

The settlement had electricity, but the residents could not afford to pay hydro bills, so the gravel road winding through Dene Village was dark on moonless nights. In summer, puddles formed around all the houses because the muskeg never drained; the drainage ditches on both sides of the gravel road became cesspools. Garbage collected outside.

Dene Village was just under a kilometre south of Akudlik, which was a well-supplied, well-maintained Inuit community with streetlights, sewage, and running water. The provincial Department of Northern Affairs had built Akudlik and maintained it. An Akudlik resident once even boasted to a community development worker that whenever a drunk person broke a window, the government made sure it was repaired the next day.[5] To the Sayisi Dene, the contrast between Dene Village and Akudlik became a symbol of injustice. At Dene Village, the suffering of the Sayisi Dene became unbearable.

Only ten short years before the establishment of Dene Village, the Sayisi Dene had been an independent and self-reliant people whose children were well cared for. Now, they were broken:

> Men who only a few years ago hunted caribou and travelled for days on end by dog team in the intense cold of the barrens and boreal forests, looking for furs and fish, now sit at home helpless and embittered. . . . Those who have seen a man in his prime become helpless as progress phased out the only work for which he was technically and psychologically prepared, may have some inkling of what it has meant for the people at Dene to lose, within a decade, most of their old way of life.[6]

Some of the outsiders who worked closely with the Dene commented on the terrible alienation that now existed between parents and their children:

> There's such a fine line between love and hate. Those Dene kids in Churchill — at times they hated their parents. I've watched kids beat their parents up, steal from

their parents. The parents were scared of those kids. I remember this one girl was at my house one evening. Her mother came to the door, drunk. I said, "Mary, go home." She didn't. Her kid shoved her off the step and jumped on her. Two months later, that mother froze to death. The guilt and the pain that kid had to live through! (Martha Commodore)

In 1968, community development worker Phil Dickman wrote:

There is practically nothing today that binds the children to their parents and pre-pares them to carry adult responsibilities. Parents and children live in different worlds and are so alienated that they often have little apparent concern or regard for each other. In reality, both are lost in a world they did not create and in which the old ways of relating are often inadequate. . . . The adolescent does not become a man by proving his prowess with gun, trap, and fish net. He knows little about these things. Instead, he becomes a man by emulating the drinking patterns of his parents."[7]

But the children who sometimes raged against their parents also tried to protect them. Phil Dickman remembers frequently seeing children leading their drunk parents or grandparents home. This would happen especially in the winter, during blizzards.

Archaeologist and anthropologist Virginia Petch, who prepared a report on the Sayisi Dene for the Royal Commission on Aboriginal Peoples in 1994, sadly com-mented, "Families disintegrated into groups of strangers[,] and elders passed away humiliated and broken hearted. What had once been a proud, industrious people was now a hopeless collection of broken people."[8]

The settlement was like a war zone. "In Dene Village, the loud noises of people fighting and shouting would start in the early evening. It was like a war. Awful. Everyone was drunk. But when you got used to that kind of chaos, it seemed natural. Instead of being scared, you became part of the destruction" (Caroline Yassie). In every house, men were abusing their wives. Rapes and beatings were daily events. Acts of brutality became commonplace. In January 1967, a drunk twenty-nine-year-old man poured coal oil on his common-law wife and set fire to her. After seeing the injured woman in hospital, someone who had had wartime experience described her injuries as the worst case of injury to a face and head that he had ever seen.[9]

As in a war zone, people were hungry and their lives were in danger. Caroline Bjorklund, a Dene woman who was married to a Métis man and who lived away from Dene Village, describes a winter day when she went to Dene Village to visit her mother. She went to see her cousin, whom she knew had just had a baby. The house was ice cold, and all the adults had passed out. The baby was on the floor, in frozen diapers and feverish with pneumonia. If Bjorklund hadn't found her when she did, she likely would have died. Many babies did die in similar circumstances.

ILA BUSSIDOR

Our house was the second one that they moved to Dene Village. The very first house they moved was the Powderhornes'. Then, our house was jacked up and moved. It was in late fall. We stayed at my granny Betsy's place in Camp-10 for a couple of days.

There were trees in the new location, so my mom and dad went to chop firewood in those first days. They weren't drinking because we were far away from town. There was still nobody else there yet, except this one other family. My mom made bannock for us. At night, it was windy and pitch black outside, but the house was warm and lit by a kerosene lamp.

It took about two weeks for everyone else to move from Camp-10 to Dene Village. Around that time, it became easier for people to go to town because a bus started to come to the corner of the road, on the hour, every hour. My parents were drinking again, and so was everyone else. The drinking got worse and worse.

When we first moved to Dene Village, I felt it would be a better life, a new life. I was happy that we were leaving Camp-10. I didn't know what was in store. I didn't know that the four short years until 1971 would be worse than any other time. Many, many people died in Dene Village.

When you came into Dene Village, there was a phone booth on the road, and from there, the road forked. The trail that veered off to the left was named Herriot Crescent, and the other one was Fowley Drive — I have no idea where they got those names. The houses were raised on four-foot-high cement foundations; they looked like they were on stilts. Almost all the windows were broken — all you needed was one beer bottle to go through those picture windows and then you had nothing but plastic or cardboard. Rags stuck out of holes in doors — doorknobs were broken. In front of most houses there was a forty-five-gallon gas barrel overflowing with garbage. Pieces of glass from broken beer and wine bottles were scattered all over the gravel pads surrounding the houses. In summer, there were puddles of stagnant, smelly water on the ground. The drainage ditches on both sides of the road got all clogged up with garbage.

A truck with a big barrel on top would come around to Dene Village to spray some stuff — it must have been an insecticide. There would be this big, smelly steam coming out of it, like a fog. We, the kids, would run into that fog until our heads were soaking with this greasy stuff. Afterwards we would all be dizzy. It seemed exciting to do that. Some adults tried to stop us, saying that the fog was poison. We never listened to them. Sometimes our parents saw us running around that truck and dragged us away from there. I still don't know what that stuff was — DDT maybe?

Children played on the gravel road. In good weather you'd see people sitting outside, in the shade of makeshift teepees. On Sundays, when they were sober, they'd make campfires beside the houses and boil tea. They also cooked on campfires when they had anything to cook — bannock or fried eggs. There was a lot of noise in Dene Village. You could hear people talking, shouting, laughing, screaming, and swearing. Those noises rose above the constant buzz of mosquitoes in summer and the whistling of the wind in winter.

In winter there was so much snow that it often covered the windows. Kids used to slide down the snowbanks. I remember a lot of blizzards when you couldn't walk because you couldn't see anything. Sometimes after a storm, a big snowblower would come to Dene Village. I remember when it came we were really excited because we always ran into the white cloud of blowing snow coming out of it.

In winter the houses were cold — maybe because of those four-foot-high cement foundations. The floors weren't insulated — they would be frozen solid. You couldn't walk around in your house in bare feet. Every house was freezing when you got up in the morning. It took maybe an hour of blazing fire to warm it up, and how can you get a blazing fire going without fuel? The government started to bring in coal once a month. When the coal was gone, you started to tear down the houses. If there was an abandoned house, it would be torn down for fuel within days. Sometimes people began to tear down their own houses.

The ceramic toilets were useless. Some people used them till they got full and then left them frozen. Eventually the people removed many of them, leaving a gaping hole on the floor of each house.

Inside, the houses were in shambles. People didn't have furniture, just beds and maybe a table and some beat-up chairs. There was almost nothing that wasn't broken or damaged. We used old jam jars as cups. We had two or three chipped plates, odd pieces of cutlery, no appliances. Nobody owned much. I remember kids coming to our door and saying, "My mom wants to borrow a knife," or an ax or scissors. Sometimes we didn't have what they were asking for. I remember one family where the kids would be fighting over a piece of bannock. If they had a little bit of sugar, they hid it from each other. There wasn't enough food.

The highlight of every month was the nineteenth — the day when people received their family allowances. We all looked forward to that day, when most kids would be wearing new running shoes and even new jeans. I remember buying crayons and a colouring book on family allowance day. That's what I bought whenever I had a little money.

My mom would take me with her to the S & M store to buy some basic food — flour, sugar, tea, maybe some pork chops. There was a handsome young Métis man in the meat department. I had to translate for my mom, and I was shy. The man would wrap the pork chops in brown paper, and after that if my mom had any money left over, she would buy a case of wine and we would take a cab home.

During our first days at Dene Village, there was electricity. But people couldn't pay hydro bills, so one by one, the houses lost their lights. After that, people would burn kerosene lamps or candles. If you didn't have those, you would melt some grease — like lard — and cut up a piece of rag two or three inches square, and roll it up and soak it in that grease. My mother used to do that. She would bend one end of the rag like a little leg so it wouldn't fall over, and she would light it. I remember all this black smoke coming out of that rag, but the black smoke would burn away in a while and you would have a candle.

On most days, people started to drink by about two o'clock in the afternoon. By evening, as they began to fight and scream, the noises increased. You would see people chasing someone, or cursing loudly. You'd hear a loud crash — somebody breaking a window. Cabs would be coming in and out of the community as people unloaded cases of beer into their houses.

We, the kids, would watch to see where those cabs went and who took how much booze into their house. We would wait until they passed out and then we would go and steal their booze. We were running around all night long as cars and cops came in and out of Dene Village. We were all part of the scene.

There were one or two days of the week when people were sober, those were Sunday and Monday. During those two short days, people would be recovering from their hangovers and trying to gather the pieces of their lives and then they would start all over again.

We were on the road to alcoholism by the time we were ten or eleven. It was the same for all the kids in Dene Village. I remember playing that we were drunk. We would put tea in a wine bottle and carry it around and fall all over the place because this was the stuff that we had seen. We were like miniatures of our parents.

The kids hung around in packs for protection. We were scared of drunk men. Some of the kids would get drunk and attack other kids. We were also afraid of being raped. When a woman passed out, there would be young boys who came along and stripped her and took turns on her. That was a common thing. Nobody was safe. It was not a pretty sight that you saw in Dene Village.

In most of my memories, I am running, running with the other kids, running all the time, running away from the truant officer, running away from drunk people, running away from Cree kids, running to find a warm place for shelter. I was scared most of the time.

The first summer at Dene Village, I was just twelve years old. One beautiful warm day in July of 1967, around mid-afternoon, my parents were already drinking with some people. I did my chores as quickly as I could so that I could go and play with my friends outside. I finally got out of the house and walked down the street looking for other kids to play with. The only person on the road was a Dene man walking towards me. He was about twenty-five years old, or older. He stopped me and when I tried to walk around him he started blocking my way. I stopped. I could tell right away he had been drinking, but he wasn't drunk. He knew what he was doing. I don't know what he said to me or what I answered, but I was lured behind a house. The next thing I knew he slugged me in the face. He kept slugging me till I blacked out.

When I came to, my head was spinning and I couldn't see. The man was gone. When I tried to stand up I kept falling, and then I noticed he had ripped off my clothes. They were scattered on the ground. Right away I knew that something really bad had happened to me. A feeling of shame and guilt came over me. Dizzy and trembling, I got dressed. I was crying. Why did no one hear me or see what had just happened to me? I was an innocent little girl. I waited a little for the dizziness to pass and snuck behind the bushes and ran across the street to my parents' house and crawled under the house and went into a corner. All the houses in Dene Village sat on cement foundations about three feet high. I remember sitting there and crying and being scared, knowing that this awful thing had happened to me. I felt blood on my thighs, and my eyes and lips were swollen from the blows of his fist. I felt dirty, and I wanted to die before anyone found out. I sat there for hours, listening to what was going on inside my parents' house. All the people in there were drunk, my mom and dad were screaming and arguing, and I just sat there not knowing what to do or where to turn. I must have fallen asleep because when I woke up it was night time. I couldn't hear any sounds from inside the house, so I crawled out from under the house and went inside. Sure enough, my mom and dad had passed out. I went into one of the rooms and dug inside my sister's suitcase. I found a bag that had underwear in it. I took out some clean underwear and took off the bloodstained ones I had on and threw them in the stove. I changed all my clothes and threw them all in the stove. I then crawled into bed and wrapped myself up so that no one could see me. I lay there and cried myself to sleep.

The next morning all the kids were supposed to go to Camp Nanook, a summer camp run by the provincial government, one of the few good things I remember about Churchill. For two weeks we would go fishing and play all kinds of games away from the misery in Dene Village. My little sister and I were ready to go. We had prepared and packed our bags days in advance. We had looked forward to this day since school was out. We were excited, and on this day the bus was coming to pick us up. That morning I was awake already when my little sister came to wake me up and get me out of bed, but I wouldn't move. I pretended to be asleep. I stayed curled up in a blanket. She said, "Ila, get up, the bus is going to come pretty soon, we gotta go." I just lay there. Finally the bus came and my little sister tried hard to drag me out of bed but I just lay there not moving. I stayed in bed all that day but I wasn't sleeping.

As the day went on, my mother began to worry about me and said, "What is wrong with that kid? She hasn't been up yet." One of my older brothers came into the room and ripped the blanket away. He held my shoulders and forced me to turn to him. He said, "Holy shit, what happened to you?" My face was swollen like a balloon. I was all bruised up. I lied right away, I said that a bunch of kids stole some booze the night before and got into a fight and I didn't remember what happened to me. My brother let me go and I lay in bed all day. Finally, when people went out to start their drinking that day, I got up and washed my face and had something to eat. I hid in that room. My brother returned during that day, and he lifted me up and sat me on the counter where I was at eye level with him. He made me look at him and he said, "Tell me the truth, what happened to you?" I repeated the same story. He didn't believe me. He knew something worse had happened, but he couldn't get it out of me.

The shame stayed with me as I grew up and became a teenager. I always felt that I was to blame for what had happened. I thought sex was an awful, dirty thing, which only bad people took part in. The sexual assault against me at this young age has altered my life in many ways and still affects me to this day as a woman. I have developed behaviour patterns that were abusive and damaging to myself. That experience has impaired my ability to develop a healthy relationship involving intimacy and sexuality as an adult. I have felt very low about myself. I used to think that I was very ugly and dirty, and I reinforced this negative self-image for years.

To this day, I experience the pain of this brutal attack. It has caused emotional, psychological, and physical damage to my spirit. Today, I see pictures of myself as a young girl, a beautiful face looking back at me, and it's hard to imagine that it was really me, someone who still lives within my soul. I want desperately to turn back time and help her, and tell her that she is not responsible for having been victimized in an environment that was not created by her or her people.

We, the children, stayed out so late that we witnessed many events that took place after dark. While they were building Dene Village, there was a big carpentry camp where the workers stayed. They were outsiders, white men. I remember how some of them used to help themselves sexually to any Dene woman who was drunk. Even if it was an old woman, they didn't care as long as they raped her and dumped her. I remember how those carpenters would come home with cases and cases of beer, and we used to see them going into their truck and driving around the village slowly, looking for drunk women. They would pick somebody up off the street and take her into that building where they stayed.

I remember car loads of white people would come to Dene Village. They would drive around looking at the people. Some of these guys would come at night. I remember seeing two girls get picked up and dragged into a van where there were about ten men. The men were heading to a place called Goose Creek, about ten kilometres down the road. They were going to rape the girls. As the car was speeding out of the village, one of the girls must have kicked the door hard, and she came rolling out on the road. She had jumped out, thrown herself out of the moving car. The car took the other girl to Goose Creek and she was raped. After the men were finished with her, they dumped her at Dene Village. We were still outside then, we saw the whole thing. She never laid charges.

Young men — army guys or just white guys — would come to Dene Village in the wee hours of the morning, they would grab one of the young girls and drag her into the car. There would be maybe eight or ten guys in the car. They would drive up to Goose Creek and rape the girl. They would return in a while and dump the girl by the phone booth. She would slump there, or stagger away. This was Dene Village.

We sometimes watched people getting into a cab. When the cab drove away, we would break into the house and steal their booze. I used to think it was really exciting to drink — the most natural thing to do. I remember that cheap wine — it was called Jordan wine — in a green bottle. When we got our hands on one of those bottles, we would stand around in a circle behind a house or in the bush somewhere, and we would pass it around. Everybody would take a big shot and swallow it. I'll never forget the taste and the smell of that wine as long as I live. It was strong and rough. When we got black-out drunk, we would fall all over the place. Many times when we drank like that, we young girls would get beaten up. Or somebody would come and rape us while we were drunk — take advantage of us as if we were animals.

As a teenager, I remember getting drunk and passing out and having men take advantage of me. I remember waking up knowing that somebody had raped me, and that sick mixture of disgust and shame would come over me. I would clean myself and hide. I wouldn't go anywhere for a long time. The shame would fade away only when I got drunk. That was a common thing in Dene Village. Other kids our age who knew about these assaults would talk about us as whores, and that increased our shame.

From those years in Churchill, I have memories of a couple of outsiders whose kindness made a difference in our lives. There was an Anglican minister named Mr. Patterson. He had a little white car that would appear on the road turning into the village on weekend afternoons. We would be hanging around outside, a pack of kids, doing nothing. He would stop by the side of the road and ask us if we wanted to go to St. Paul's Church downtown to play some games. He would drive around the village and pile up the kids in his car and take us to the Anglican church. There, he would offer us juice and cookies, he would tell us stories from the Bible, show us pictures, try to teach us songs and play ping-pong with us. He was a kind man. If we fought with each other or fooled around noisily, he would try to get us in line, but he couldn't. We liked him and we took advantage of him in a harmless kind of way. He would tell us to listen to him. I remember looking forward to going to St. Paul's Church with him because it was fun.

After a couple of hours, he usually drove us back home. I remember how we fooled around in the back of his little car. He always offered to drop off each one of us beside our houses. But we preferred to get off at one place so we could bumper-shine — drag on the ice behind his car. As soon as he was beginning to drive away we would grab the back of his car. He knew we were doing it. He would slam on his brakes and come out to see all these kids, about ten of us, hanging on to his car. He had these slip-on rubbers on his shoes. He would take one off and run after us, shouting, "Don't do that, you could get killed," pretending he would paddle our bums. And then he'd get back in his car and we would run and hang on to his car again. We did that until he drove away from Dene Village.

We did that to buses or cabs that came to Dene Village too. Some kids dragged behind a bus or a cab for eight kilometres to the army camp [called Camp]. That was a way of getting to Camp to a show. Once, some kids were doing that and one of the wheels slipped and ran over a girl's head, but she wasn't seriously hurt.

And then there was Martha Commodore, a community development worker who came to Dene Village around 1968. She actually lived in Dene Village. Martha visited people in their houses without making them feel intruded on. When someone's kids were apprehended she tried to intervene on behalf of the family. She started a girls' club for us. She taught us how to bake, how to cook some simple things. We would go to her house and bake cakes and cookies to sell on Treaty Days, and she put that money in the bank to cover some of the expenses of Camp Nanook — the summer camp. Martha's house was always open to us. Sometimes, when we were hungry, she offered us food. Once a week, we all went to her place for a bath. Martha would ask some of the older girls to help wash the hair of younger ones like me. Sometimes Martha would cut our hair or our nails. If anyone had lice in their hair, Martha had some stuff to treat it. On Thursday nights, she got us together to watch a movie or play some games. She was someone I felt safe with. I knew she cared about me and about the other kids.

She gave the young girls in Dene Village an important message with the things she did with us and for us. She talked to us about sex and about sexually transmitted diseases. She tried to make us feel that we were valuable and that we could support each other.

ERNIE BUSSIDOR

I came home from the show at Camp one day, and my house wasn't there in Camp-10. It was a cold, moonlit night around Halloween. There wasn't much snow yet, that year. Someone told me they had just jacked up the house and moved it to the new location. That's how they had moved the houses — just put them on semi-trailers, on low-boys, and transported them.

I think the community really turned in on itself when we got to Dene Village. All of a sudden we were alone. We weren't exposed to scrutiny from anybody. People started to destroy each other instead of just destroying themselves.

Despite everything that was going on around me, I went to school every day. The school bus would appear on that gravel road in the morning, and all those kids got on it, no matter what kind of a night they'd had, whether they had a hangover or not. When the truant officer saw a kid on the street, he would grab him, throw him in the car and take him to school. We got strapped regularly. Some of us wouldn't even have our faces washed. We wore mismatched socks, and dirty, tattered clothes — a lot of dirty-faced kids in dirty clothes. Sometimes these kids didn't eat, or they didn't sleep the night before, or else they slept on the street. If you saw a kid in the classroom with his hair sticking up with dirty feathers in it and smelly clothes — maybe he was at the dump the day before, playing in the tire yard or something. You could see the degradation of the environment we lived in by looking at the children.

In the mid-sixties, the Department of Indian Affairs organized a lunch program at the St. Paul's Anglican Mission. I remember chicken noodle soup and baloney sandwiches. All the Cree kids used to go there too. There were more of the Cree kids than us, and they used to bully us. But the lunch program didn't last long because the Anglican church didn't have enough volunteers to keep preparing the soup and the sandwiches.

Our local lay reader, John Clipping, was one of the few people in Dene Village who didn't drink. He took over the responsibility of making sandwiches for us. He would gather the kids in his house and let them make their own sandwiches, jam sandwiches — frozen butter on bread, and jam. A box full of those sandwiches would be on the bus in the morning, sometimes with some apples. You get sick of jam after a while, so we used to go to the back of Hudson's Bay or the S & M store and maybe find a box full of half-decent bananas and fill up on bananas.

Behind the Churchill grain elevator, they used to have a cook house for the harbour workers. We used to go there for leftovers. They would make a vat of twenty-five gallons of soup or something like that. There was always five or six gallons left over after lunch. They would bring that out. People used to go there with pails or tin cans. I had my own tin can in a little hiding place in the willows. I would bring that out and wait in line. Some days you could get a gallon of soup — other days maybe five pounds of mashed potatoes.

When more people found out about this place, there were mobs — maybe fifty, sixty people at lunch time, so they stopped serving leftover food to us and we started breaking into their garbage bin. They started locking the garbage bin with a lock and key, and we would still break in there anyway.

I remember a dark summer night when there were about ten or fifteen of us hungry kids. We broke into the cook-shack dumpster. My friend Tommy Mowatt dug into this one bag, and he yelled, "Holy smokes, mashed potatoes!" He grabbed this big, heavy garbage bag and started running off into the willows. Three or four boys followed him, but he told them to get lost because he wasn't sharing this with anybody. He got to the edge of the willows and he dug into his bag. Soon he came out looking sheepish. He had to tell us there were wet napkins in that bag.

The next night, we went back to the cook-shack dumpster and in the darkness we ate what we found. Sometimes my stomach started to churn, but that's how we lived.

We, the boys, lived fantasy lives through the movies. Gladiators and Western heroes were our idols. *Spartacus. The Good, the Bad and the Ugly.* When we sat in a darkened theatre at Camp and watched Tony Curtis or Kirk Douglas or Clint Eastwood on the screen, our world was transformed. The adults loved it too. Every Sunday, there'd be a bus picking up people in Dene Village, and they would fill up that bus, to go to the movies. The Sunday movie was the highlight of our days.

I remember a bunch of us boys scraping and scrounging to raise five dollars to buy a .22 single-shot cadet rifle from the local pawnbroker, Windy Smith. We began to hunt ptarmigans with that. We also made little (two feet wide and three feet long) toboggans. We made a network of trails with our little toboggans. A resourceful bunch — but we were already alcoholics.

I remember Christmas 1971 — it was bitterly cold. The band used to organize an annual Christmas dinner at the band hall. That year a lot of people were drunk, there were hardly any volunteers. They hired five or six of us kids to go with our toboggans and hand out these turkeys to people who were supposed to cook them [for the community dinner]. You could fit three turkeys in a box on a little toboggan and pull it with runners. So we delivered all these turkeys, about twenty of them, to people that had oven-stoves.

Later that afternoon, just before dark, we had to collect those turkeys. There was a lot of drinking going on. When we got the birds back, some of them were half-cooked, some of them were half eaten. We had to wrestle them out of these homes and put them on our toboggans and haul them over to the hall for the Christmas dinner. I remember it was a sad Christmas. That dinner was the only event that marked the holiday. There were no presents in the homes. The kids never got anything, ever.

I remember one day at Christmas, we were standing inside the S & M store. My grandpa went to the liquor store to buy some wine. We were waiting for a taxi. I remember my granny was standing there, looking out the window. And I saw that there were tears in her eyes. For some reason, I dwelled on that for a long time. I couldn't figure out why my granny was standing there, crying. Once when I was drunk, I confronted her. I thought she was crying because she was getting old. All she said was no, that wasn't the reason. Maybe it was the kind of life we lived at that time.

We had very little to wear. A lot of kids had cold feet and cold hands. I used to wear five, six socks on top of each other. We knew how to walk to Camp along the highway without freezing to death. We also did a lot of bumper-shining — that was our favourite mode of travelling in winter when the roads were covered with ice and we could slide on them.

You would see all these Dene kids lined up at the last bus stop in town heading up the highway to Camp. If a passenger was getting on, we would all line up behind the bus and bumper-shine all the way to Dene Village or from Camp to Akudlik.

I remember the buses going seventy, eighty miles an hour, while the drivers knew there were kids back there. One time there was a scary incident.

We were all sitting on the bus, and Buddy, one of the boys, had no bus fare so he was hanging on to the back of the bus. All you could see through the blowing snow was this little ball underneath the bus. Suddenly, there was a five-ton moving-and-storage truck right behind the bus. Buddy couldn't let go. The truck followed the bus all the way from downtown to Akudlik. The bus turned in to Akudlik and the big truck went zipping by, and you could see Buddy just rolling across the road.

The night time was when people really came out in Dene Village, even in winter. We used to walk to Camp sometimes in winter time. Holy smokes! Polar bear season too. Everybody always kept a wary eye out for polar bears. People used to go to the dump and see polar bears foraging twenty feet away from them. You got along with polar bears, as long as you didn't dig in the same pile or fight over the same piece of meat.

I remember when a polar bear came into Dene Village. They said a woman just walked out on her front steps and ran into the animal. Her brother came out and started kicking at the bear. He was drunk. The bear ripped that guy's skull cap and all the flesh down his back and left him in a bloody heap there and bit the woman in the waist and he was carrying her away. Two of the young men in Dene Village heard the screams and they shot the bear. Peter or Alex, whoever shot the bear, must have been a good shot because it was in the dark and there were people around, but he saved the lives of that woman and her brother.

We, the young teenagers, were becoming an uncontrollable mob. We went through the phases of sniffing, alcohol, tobacco, violence, gang rapes, and beatings. We had our scapegoats. There was one family we picked on regularly, I don't know why. We ransacked their home. We broke into their house and demolished their things many times. We threw rocks at them.

We had a way of breaking into every home in Dene Village. Every house was like a barricaded fortress. The windows, if they weren't smashed up and covered with polyethylene, would be covered with a metal grate. Doors would have three or four locks on them. But there was a way into every house.

That way was through the attic hole. You could crawl in through the attic vents and crawl in through the attic hole, and you would be standing in the middle of the house. The doors were barricaded by logs and stuff people found at the dump site.

We were also pretty adept at stealing. We got into the habit of breaking into businesses, hotels where there was alcohol. We were always looking for alcohol. If there was no alcohol, then we would settle for food. We were scorned by the townsfolk: "The dirty little bastards in Dene Village." We weren't allowed anywhere in many of the stores. If we walked into a store, the security people there would make sure we were thrown out.

There is an incident that still shocks me to this day. It was in January 1969. A very, very cold Friday night getting into early Saturday morning. We were walking around. We had shut down the main power box to Dene Village because we had found the main power switch. We shut off all the lights in the village. Not very many people had hydro anyway. Nobody had any appliances.

So, we're walking down the road, a whole mob of us. I was about twelve. Some boys in the group were fourteen, fifteen. We're kind of gathering in force there. We met this woman who might have been in her late thirties. For some reason we started taunting her. We got aggressive and started to molest her right on the street. She was scared. It was such a cold night, fifty below maybe. Somehow, things started getting kinda weird and she ended up on the road. We had completely stripped her. She was telling us to leave her alone. We were kinda laughing at her. I think she was sober.

All of this was happening in front of the house of an old woman named Eva. Somehow she came out and chased us away and took this woman into her house. We had a laugh about it at that time, but if Eva hadn't come out, that woman would have died on the road.

Those kinds of things almost started to become normal for us.

When I was fifteen years old — a little, scrawny guy — I was thrown into jail one night. It was New Year's Eve, 1971. There was a big party at the band hall. Somehow I had been drinking before I went there, and when I got there, there was a commotion. There had been a knife fight outside, some guy had been stabbed, and the cops had arrived. By the time I walked in there, some people were running away.

The cops started to round up the people, and somehow I got thrown into the paddy wagon; I didn't know what was happening. At the police station, they threw me into the juvenile side.

The adult cell was across from the juvenile cell. In there, there were five or six white boys. Big, tough, menacing guys. They had crashed a house party somewhere in Churchill and they were thrown in jail. They were drunk and upset to be in jail.

Five Chipewyan adults were thrown in the same cell. They huddled underneath the bunk beds there. While I stood looking at them, the white rednecks began to beat them up. They tortured those poor guys all night.

In my cell there were two white boys and one bunk bed. I went to sleep on the floor under the bunk bed. I woke up in the middle of the night. Somehow, somebody had been beating me — because I woke up with black, swollen eyes, a broken nose, and a fat lip. Out of one eye, I couldn't see. My face was pulverized. Those two boys in the cell were both in my age group, they were in my class in school. When they woke up, nobody said a word. I didn't have the courage or the dignity to even look at anybody. I was under the bed, watching the adults getting beaten up on the other side, and I just more or less figured that's what had happened to me, that the two boys in my cell had beaten me up.

I don't know why, I was one of the last ones to get released from jail on January 1, 1972. On the adult side, my late uncle, Jimmy, was the last guy coming out. They gave me back my scruffy old parka. I remember how terrible I felt — I was all beaten. I didn't know what I looked like. There was blood on my face.

There was a whiteout that night, a blizzard. When you looked out the door of the cop station, you couldn't see anything, just a white wall. The highway to Dene Village was closed. No vehicles were running.

One of the white boys must have stolen my shoes, I had only socks on. I could hardly speak but I told the police, "I can't find my boots." The cop looked at me. "Well, buddy," he said, "you can either go back to your cell or hit the road. You don't have much choice." "I'm not going to stay here another minute," I said. I walked out and waited for Jimmy. Just then they called him back: "You forgot something here." It was a twenty-six-ounce Canadian Club. He had been thrown in jail with his precious bottle in his jacket pocket. I hadn't been very optimistic that I could make it home alive, barefoot in the sub-arctic January blizzard outside the jail house that day. But when the cops gave Jimmy that bottle back, I remember I had a glimmer of hope — that maybe we would make it.

Jimmy was a short guy. He gave me the duffel liners from his size-six shoes. (My feet were size nine.) We hit the snowbank. We managed to work our way down to the other end of Hudson Square. We got onto the highway and headed up towards the end of town. You couldn't see anything in the whiteout. The wind and snow were roaring in our faces. There were no vehicles anywhere. We stumbled along in the snow. When we got near the arena, I told Jimmy to open up that bottle. My feet were cold.

When there's a blizzard in Churchill, there's nothing to prevent the snow from collecting in heaps. No trees, no tall buildings to cut the wind, so it just blows. We got to the highway and kept drinking out of that bottle. By the time we got to the bend in the road that goes to the navy base, I was pretty high. I had no hat, no mitts, no shoes, and I was beaten black and blue, and I kept walking.

I don't remember walking into the house. I know my granny was shocked as I came into the doorway. I just passed out. That was a Friday night — New Year's Day.

On Monday, I put on a pair of sun glasses. My swollen lip was beginning to go down. I had picked the scabs off my face. I went back to school.

After we moved to Dene Village, a community development worker named Harry Steen started a boys' club for us. He would rent movies and show them to us on Wednesday nights. Somehow, Steen got hockey sticks for us — and the kids really got into it. We played road hockey from dawn till dusk. When the schools were closed because the wind chill was 2,600 and there was a blizzard, all these boys were outside playing road hockey.

When Harry Steen left Dene Village, an unimposing bearded guy named Phil

Dickman showed up to replace him. Our initial reaction to Phil was, "Who the hell is this guy?" He was a social worker who worked for the province. He became our friend. Phil got us into hockey, baseball — he tried to get us involved with the community of Churchill. In the summer, he would get us to wash windshields and things like that. He worked above the post office on the second floor. The post office was off limits to us, but we could always go upstairs and visit Phil Dickman. Five, six, seven of us, however many of us there were. He invited us to his office. He just opened his door to us. He made us coffee and offered us digestive cookies. A day wouldn't go by when we didn't visit him.

Hockey became almost a fever. In Churchill, winter lasts for nine months out of a year. Every night we played road hockey.

Phil managed to get some kind of a donation from Winnipeg, some organization provided us all with skates. I must have been eleven or twelve. There were about twenty of us. Phil used to take us to the arena on Saturday mornings. We never knew how to skate until then. It took us a while to get the hang of it. We learned how to skate on the pond. Phil got us to play hockey with the pee-wee league in town, with the white kids and the other Native kids. We were playing with five-, six-, seven-year-olds. It was the first time we were actually in the arena, on the ice, playing hockey. It was fun.

The arena was a popular place for the community of Churchill. With the army, the navy, and the air force there, there was some good hockey, but we weren't part of any of that — we would have been sneaking around there looking for cigarette butts — until Phil got us playing.

Phil Dickman gave us a feeling of connectedness. A sense that we shouldn't just get together to drink and get into trouble, that there were other things.

MARY YASSIE

A regular evening in Camp-10 and Dene Village was always the same. The noise was unbelievable. You could hear the people yelling and fighting, and the taxis that came in and out of the community were non-stop. The kids would be watching the cabs and who brought booze into their homes, and we would wait and then break into the houses after the adults passed out, and we would steal all the booze we could find. All or most of the kids were well on their way to alcoholism already and we would do whatever it took to get the booze. Most of the homes in Dene Village were wrecked. The windows had gaping holes in them with rags hanging out to keep the wind out. Nobody had glass on their windows. Either the adults that were fighting broke them or it was the kids. It just didn't matter any more how we lived.

Most homes had stoves that were given to us by the Department of Indian Affairs, but what was the use of having woodstoves when there was no firewood for heat? There was never enough food for the kids. We were always hungry. Today I tell my children that if my late dad hadn't walked to the garbage dump and brought home slices of bread crust and scrap meat, you wouldn't be here today. This is the honest truth. The way that most of the kids dressed was always in tattered clothes, in the winter we didn't have proper footwear, we always wore cheap running shoes, and we were always cold. It's a wonder that we never froze our feet or hands. It's hard to believe that the kids survived those long winters in Churchill. I never want to see my children go through something like that, not in my lifetime.

While we were living in Dene Village, my parents were raising my older sister's two kids. After my sister died from alcohol, my parents took the two small children. One day someone from the Children's Aid came over to our house and made my parents sign forms without letting them know what they were signing. They were home alone and no one was there to translate for them. They were tricked into signing adoption forms for their two small grandchildren. One day they came and took those two children away and we have never seen them to this day. We don't know what happened to them. Kids were always taken away from the homes like this. If my parents had a translator they would never have signed forms like that. They would never think of it. My parents were good people when they were sober.

There were many times when people would break into each other's homes looking for booze and beat up whoever was home. This one time some young guys came into our house and beat up my dad for no reason at all. He was beaten so bad that he had internal bleeding and needed emergency surgery. He was hospitalized for months after that. Another time during the winter my mother came home and said, "Your dad fell down on the road, he's too drunk to walk, come and help me bring him in the house." My brothers and I went out to look for him. We went in different directions and finally found him crawling on the road. He was drunk and his hands were frozen. If my mother had been black-out drunk, my dad would have frozen to death on the streets of Dene Village that night. The doctor told my dad that if the palms of his hands had frozen, then they would have had no choice but to amputate his fingers. He was lucky he didn't lose his fingers.

My brother Walter and I looked after my grandmother when we lived in Camp-10. She was very old and blind. My dad built a small shack for her next to our house. It was one room with a small bed and a homemade stove inside. This is where she lived until she died. If it wasn't for me, my grandmother would never have survived those long cold winter nights in Churchill. I used to keep the fire going, burning old rags and whatever scraps I could find. When the old-age security pension cheques would come in, my brother Walter and I would take my granny to town. We would hitch these two dogs onto a small sled and take her to the post office and then to the S & M supermarket to buy groceries. Her pension cheque was always seventy-five dollars. It seemed like a lot of money. My poor granny was lost in this drunken mess. Nobody paid any attention to her needs except for me. I became her caregiver. I was just a young kid.

By the end of the sixties, a generation of Sayisi Dene teenagers who grew up in the chaos of the abrupt transition from life on the land to life in the slums was approaching adulthood. A handful among them graduated from Churchill's junior high school in the spring of 1971. Ila Bussidor was one of them.

ILA BUSSIDOR

About five girls and six boys had not dropped out, somehow. Graduation was approaching, and of course we didn't have dresses or shoes to go to the graduation. At the time, a man named Les Oslund, who was sensitive to the Sayisi Dene, was Indian agent. He, his wife, Doreen, and a woman named Dee Summerville, whose husband was working for the Manitoba Indian Brotherhood, wanted us, the Dene Village kids, to take part in that community celebration. They made it happen for us.

I remember the day when Dee and Doreen took us to the store to pick out materials and patterns that we wanted for graduation dresses — I don't know how they put together the money, it must have come from the Department of Indian Affairs. We bought all this stuff, fabric for dresses, shoes, nylons, everything. Then we, five young girls who were graduating, spent about two weeks with those two ladies who sewed dresses for all of us. We helped them, but they did it. I'll never forget the colour of the dress that I had: cranberry satin! On the day of the graduation, Dee Sommerville helped us get ready. All our dresses were at her house. We all went there. They brought the boys too. They had bought ties and shirts for them. About ten to twelve of us.

They styled our hair. That was the time when "the beehive" was in style. Some of the girls had beehive hairdos. One of the girls from Dene Village was selected valedictorian. We all felt proud in our new dresses.

It was the first time that the Dene Village kids were participating in a social event in Churchill. I remember it made me feel important. I was part of something good. I was dressed like the other girls, my hair was curled and done attractively. Deep down, I felt good about it.

We all got a ride into town together. The graduation ceremony was at the old community hall in town. On both sides of the hall, tables were set with flowers and attractively arranged salads, cold cuts, and dainties. The people of Churchill — teachers, social workers, parents — and our own chief and council were sitting in rows of seats facing a stage. When our names were called we went up on that stage to get a piece of paper. I remember I was shaky. I felt beautiful, and grown up. I was getting a piece of paper that was important.

After the ceremony, there was a dinner and a dance to the tunes of the Beatles, Rolling Stones, and Credence Clearwater Revival. We all stayed. The chief and councillors were also dressed up. Late Dan Bighead was one of the councillors. I've seen pictures of him taken that day, standing in his suit jacket and his tie. My brother Horace was there, and so were Peter Thorassie and Alex Sandberry.

Afterwards, there was a bonfire on the rocks at the beach. We, the Dene Village kids, went there with all the other students. Everyone was kind and friendly to us.

We felt accepted. There were hot dogs, marshmallows, and pop. We had such a good time. Those women had made that possible for us.

That summer, Ila got a job as a Dene interpreter and nurse's aide at the Fort Churchill Hospital at the army camp. On one payday, she rushed home to give money to her parents. She remembers that afternoon:

It was a bright sunny day. Mosquitoes and black flies were buzzing. I came home in the early afternoon, and as soon as I walked in, I knew that people had been drinking in the house because it was messy. There were wine bottles, beer bottles, all over the place and nobody home.

As I stood looking around, I heard something. Someone was crying. It sounded like my mom. I didn't know where the sound was coming from. I looked in the rooms, she wasn't there. I went outside, towards the back of the house. I could still hear her crying. I looked under the house. Nothing. I stood outside and listened. The sound was coming from the direction of the railroad tracks just behind the house. I went over there. I looked up and down the railway. Then I saw her.

My mom was lying on the ground beside the railway tracks. She was crying, sobbing. I went up to her and asked her to get up. She didn't respond to me. I asked her why she was crying. She didn't answer. I sat there with her for a long time while she cried. Finally she sat up. I looked at her. She wasn't drunk. She had been drinking but she wasn't drunk.

Finally she spoke to me. "In my lifetime I worked hard," she said in Dene. "I used to go out into the bush and get wood, drag frozen logs back to our tent or cabin. I set nets for fish. I worked all the time to live and to care for my children. But the hardship of raising a family in the bush, all that toil, will have been for nothing. Nothing. The day that I lay my head down to rest, wherever that happens, it will happen in a pitiful way. It will have been all a waste."

I held her, I even rocked her gently. We sat on the railway tracks for a while. Even after she was quiet, tears ran down her face.

DEATHS

After the move to Camp-10, as alcohol became a force in their lives, the Sayisi Dene had begun to die sudden, unnatural deaths. In 1960, three young children had died in a house fire. In 1962, twenty-nine-year-old Sandy Cheekie had drowned while drunk. A year later, Betsy Anderson's sons, Jimmy and Johnny, had drowned in the Churchill River. From then on, "it was as if an unseen force was clubbing them to death" (Caroline Yassie). The people were numb with pain. "Nobody took a daily tally and said 'we've had seventy-nine deaths and counting.' Whenever a body was found, a terrible uneasiness hung over the community. People who were trapped in that existence didn't know what was happening to them" (Ernie Bussidor). But the mounting death toll crushed their spirits.

When the people moved to Dene Village, the death rate accelerated. Most of the time, people didn't have money for a bus or cab ride. They would walk home on the railway tracks, even when the temperature was minus thirty degrees, and the wind was roaring and gusting. On the way, many froze to death. Others were killed on the road in hit-and-run accidents. Babies died of tuberculosis or malnutrition. People died in house fires. People drowned in the river. People died in beatings, stabbings. "If the person who died was just a drunk Sayisi Dene walking home, it was treated as if it wasn't serious. Nobody investigated their deaths.

Nobody laid charges. Nobody compensated their families" (Ila Bussidor).

Many years later, one band member described how he had been surrounded by death. He was a little boy when three of his siblings died in a house fire at Camp-10. His mother was murdered, and the suspected killer was his father, who died from alcohol poisoning right before his eyes while the two of them were fishing in the Churchill River. His grandmother died in a house fire. His grandfather was found dead on a hill in Churchill. His nephew was found frozen to death on a beach, and his uncle was also frozen to death. His wife died from alcohol poisoning. "People just kept dying," was how he summed up his story.[1]

EVA YASSIE

My mother froze to death. I was only about eleven or twelve at the time. I believe it was in 1969. My father was in the Ninette sanatorium for tuberculosis. We didn't have a house yet so we were living with Grandma. One day, my mother got a letter from my dad. It was in syllabics so I couldn't read it. But I remember her reading that letter and crying. I knew something was wrong. She was sitting there, crying for a long time. She said Dad had accused her of fooling around with another man.

She was sewing that day. She was making slippers. She finished her slippers. She said she was going into town to sell them. She asked me, "Can you look after your brothers till I get back?" I said, "Yes." She went to town with my granny. She did sell her slippers. She came back. She had bought a little bit of food and some wine. She started drinking that wine. You could tell she was upset. As the evening wore on, she kept saying to my grandmother, "Let's go to the beer parlour." Granny didn't want to go with her. She kept bugging Granny to go. Finally Granny gave in: "Okay, I'll go with you. Not for long, though, just for a little while." So they went. They made it to town, and that's the last time Granny saw my mom.

It was in January. They had gone to the Hudson Hotel and my mom had told Granny, "Wait for me, I'll be right back." She never came back. Granny came home that evening, about nine thirty or ten. She said, "Is your mom home?" I said, "No." Granny knew right there and then. She said, "I don't think we'll ever see her again if she is not here now."

Sure enough. We got up in the morning, still no Mom. As soon as Granny got up, she got dressed and she went out. The search was on for my mom.

A man had been walking along the railway tracks from town to Dene Village — about eight kilometres. That man found her body. She had been trying to walk home, she had just fallen on the side of the tracks and frozen. Apparently she had been crying before she died. Tears had frozen on her face.

ILA BUSSIDOR

There was a boy named Edward Bighead, around eleven or twelve years old, who liked to smoke. He collected cigarette butts in front of hotels and stores downtown. From time to time, he used to take off and stay away for days.

One day he disappeared. People said he was sneaking around in the village at night, and hiding in the streets downtown. But after a while nobody saw him anymore. Some said a "hobo" had kidnapped him. In Churchill we were very scared of these bums who sneaked into town in boxcars. There were a lot of them. We called them hobos.

A couple of months later, a young Dene man who was walking from Churchill to Dene Village along the railway tracks saw a bunch of seagulls hovering over the bay. He walked over there and noticed a bad smell. There was a body there.

People had been sort of looking for Edward but there was no organized search. The body on the shore was identified by the tattoos on his hand. Sure enough, it was Edward. Nobody cared or investigated how he died. It was just another kid from Dene Village. It wasn't important.

A young girl, named Annie Yassie, went missing. She was about thirteen. She had gone into a cab with this young guy from the village. They had gone up to Goose Creek or someplace like that to drink. That's where she was last seen. They never found a trace of her. No body, nothing. The guy who had been with her was questioned and let go. Where were all the social workers and cops of Churchill? Where were the people who thought they had saved the caribou from extinction? How is it that no one cared, no one ever found out what happened to Annie Yassie?

There was a family next door to us who had a lot of children. The man was in the sanatorium for a long time. He spoke English really well. He was a handsome, tall man. I grew up with their kids. But when that man started drinking, that was one of the families that suffered a lot. He used to pound the living hell out of his wife. It seemed she always had a black eye. He froze to death in Churchill when he was drunk. Trying to come home, he must have walked off the trail into a snowbank. They found his frozen body.

The family of the man who asked the Indian agent for fuel in Camp-10 suffered a lot in Churchill, perhaps because they had so many kids. I knew those kids. They used to hide bits of sugar or pieces of bread from each other. Their father was killed on the highway in a hit-and-run accident. His body was so mangled that it was hardly recognizable. Nobody knows whether the driver was drunk. He was never charged. There was never an investigation. His wife was just left with all those children.

ERNIE BUSSIDOR

Ila Oman, my late aunt, was murdered around 1971. It was around fall time. She was a kind, sweet lady when she was sober, but when she drank she became loud and aggressive. That evening, Ila Oman came to our house in Dene Village, drunk and yelling. My granny was also drinking, and somehow they got into an argument and my granny punched her and threw her out of our house.

It must have been about an hour later that they say she ran into some kids — teenagers — who beat her. People said he had been carrying an ax and that he hit her across the head with the back of the ax. After being beaten up by kids, Ila Oman was lying on the road, and two adult men from the village thought she had just passed out, and they took her into a house, they raped her, and they threw her back out. She lay on the road for about twenty-four hours. Those guys who raped her must have known something was wrong. They — or someone else — called an ambulance. That day, Ila Oman died in the hospital.

The cops investigated and pinned it on two girls and a teenage guy, but later they dropped the charges because they didn't have enough evidence. No one knew whether it was the men who raped her or the kids who assaulted her who had dealt the blow that killed her. Some people say the men who raped her had beaten her up and she was crawling and crying on the road when the kids began to pick on her. Who knows? The RCMP questioned my granny too. My granny had a hard time forgiving herself, because Ila Oman was her niece and my granny had thrown her out that night.

EVA ANDERSON

I used to take pity on the children in Dene Village. When their parents were drunk, the children would be hungry and without a place to sleep. I would hear them crying as they were scared to go home where there were people drunk and fighting. They would be standing around the corner of my house. I would let them in and make a place for them to sleep on the floor. I didn't have much but at least they were safe inside my house. I had my own problems to deal with at that time, but at the same time I was always concerned about the poor children who were caught in the middle of this drunken mess. My heart was in pain for them. I didn't want to see children suffering, but it was an everyday thing in Dene Village.

My only daughter died in Churchill, from alcohol abuse. She froze to death while attempting to walk the five or six miles from town to Dene Village. It was like my soul died along with her, but I knew I had to be strong for my grandchildren, who were left without a mother. I was already an elder, I was no longer a young woman who can raise children. But I did, I had no choice. Today I have lived to see my great-grandchildren. Another time of great pain for me was when my granddaughter Annie went missing on a Treaty Day. She was thirteen years old. She just disappeared, maybe she was killed. Her body was never found, and to this day we don't know what happened to her. She went drinking with a man past Dene Village. That was the last anyone saw her. My brother's son, who was also just a child (between twelve and thirteen years old), also went missing from Dene Village, and his body was found on the shore of Churchill River. He was just a little boy who was running from the violence and drunken people in Dene Village. The deaths of these children were never investigated by the RCMP, the way they were supposed to be. Maybe about a week of searching, but after that it was just left unfinished.

It's sad to think of all this. When I was a young woman and before I was born, our people lived in harmony with each other and the land. The spirit of our people was happy.

The houses in Dene Village were fire traps. People burned scraps because there was no wood. With poor ventilation and fierce winds, it took no more than a spark to start a raging fire. The chimneys were always getting red hot because the stove pipes were getting burnt out and needed replacement. No one ever replaced them.

On January 29, 1971, the three youngest children of Caroline and Peter Yassie died in a house fire. It was an exceptionally cold and stormy day. There was a whiteout, which reduced visibility to under a metre. "But you could see this big orange haze to the north. The wind was so strong that some of the embers and the smoke were reaching five houses down the road. There was a lot of commotion. The parents of the children were hysterical. People were milling around, drunk" (Ernie Bussidor).

The *Taiga Times*, the Churchill newspaper, reported that the fire alarm was received by the Churchill Fire Department forty-five minutes after the flames engulfed the house. There was no telephone in Dene Village, and men had to struggle against winds gusting to about sixty-five kilometres per hour to turn the alarm in from Akudlik; just under a kilometre away. The fire truck and a grader had arrived in Dene Village about 11:55 and recovered the bodies of the three children.[2]

CAROLINE YASSIE

We had six children. We were out that night. My second oldest, Donna, woke up from the heat of the walls. The house was already on fire. She was too young to realize what was going on, but she woke up her older brother Clifford. Clifford took his brother Howard outside and came back inside to get Donna. He went back inside the house again to get his other brothers and little sister. He grabbed his five-year-old brother Michael, but Michael got out of his grip and said, "I want to wait for my mummy and daddy," and ran back into the room and closed the door.

The house was in flames. Clifford stood there and heard his little brother crying from inside his parents' room. The walls were starting to cave in and there was smoke everywhere. He ran out and in seconds the whole house blew up in flames. There were three small children trapped inside: Michael, Raymond, and Doreen, ages five to two years. Today Clifford lives with that memory. It's a great burden to carry.

After that, life became a nightmare. There was no way to stop the horror. It's very difficult to talk about all this. How I lived through these events, or why, I do not know. Even when you love people deeply, they can be taken away from you just like that, in an instant, and the pain just settles in your heart. I can't describe that pain.

After losing our three children, my husband and I separated. Clifford stayed with his father. The other two went to a home in The Pas, Manitoba. I was two months pregnant at the time of the fire. I used to wander around all over the place in Dene Village and in town, in all hours of the night. I couldn't sleep, I couldn't eat. All I did was drink, drink, drink, to hide my pain. When the baby was born seven months later, she was only three pounds. They kept her at the hospital because she was so small.

My mother used to cry when she saw me in this condition. Once I passed out on the rubble and ashes of the house where my children had died. A cab driver had seen me and got me out of there.

My husband was in the same condition, he was also hurting terribly. He was drunk, staggering on the road every time I saw him.

In the summer of 1971, a zoology professor from Guelph and his wife, who were in Churchill for research, offered Ila Bussidor a way out of Dene Village. Ron and Carole Brooks invited her to live with them in Guelph and finish high school there. Ila accepted. She felt out of place in their middle-class suburban life but gradually began to adjust. She attended a high school where she was the only Aboriginal student.

In December 1972, a week before Ila was to go home to Dene Village for Christmas, she had a frightening dream.

ILA BUSSIDOR

I was standing in a watchtower in an airport. An Air Canada plane suddenly crashed in front of me and burst into flames. I was standing behind glass, there were flames all around me. As I watched in horror, another plane went down in flames. Everything was burning, people were caught in the fire. I woke up in dread, a sick feeling in my heart.

I was looking forward to seeing my parents and my brothers and sisters. When I had that horrible dream, I told Carole Brooks I was afraid of going home. "Don't be silly," she said. "It's just a dream."

I flew from Guelph to Winnipeg and met my younger sister Marjorie there. The two of us travelled to Churchill together. Some of the people in Dene Village had left Churchill to return to the land, but my parents were still in their house. They had been preparing for us, they had cleaned the house. My mother was sewing away, making moccasins and mitts to sell for groceries and Christmas booze. I remember how happy they were to see us — and they were sober. They didn't drink at all those two days before Christmas Eve.

But everyone else in the village was drinking. The night before Christmas Eve, the man who lived with one of my older sisters came to our house, drunk. He started to beat up my sister. One of my brothers had to throw him out of the house.

My mom had made a bed for us on the floor in their bedroom. I remember coming back from outside later that night and getting ready for bed. My mom and dad were sitting on their bed, my dad was having a smoke. "Sele," he said, "my daughter, these men that live with your sisters and beat them. Don't ever let that happen to you." I wondered why he was saying this to me, because I was so young. I wasn't living with anybody. Those were his last words to me.

As they sat there, my mom asked me, "That smoke that kids are smoking around here, are you into that?" She meant pot. I lied: "No." That was the last time my mom asked me anything, the last time I heard her speak.

When I woke up the next morning, my mom and dad were already gone to town. I got out of my floor-bed, got into their bed and went back to sleep. I must have slept through the morning. It was past two o'clock when I woke up again. I ate, cleaned the house, and went out to visit friends.

Later on that evening, a group of us went to a show in Camp, about seven miles from Dene Village. In the middle of the movie, I had an uneasy feeling. I wanted to leave. I started getting up. "Let's go," I said to these girls. "Let's go." But nobody wanted to leave. They were annoyed with me because I kept getting up. I couldn't sit still. Something was telling me to leave. To go home.

After the show ended, we got on the bus to go back to Dene Village. Another girl, named Alice, got on the bus after us and she came beside us. "The bus driver said there was a house on fire in Dene Village," she said. We all thought it must be one of the empty houses at the end of the road. Some families had already moved away from the village, the empty houses were often vandalized.

Usually, when the bus got to Dene Village, it just turned around and let people out, but this time it drove all the way through the village. As it was turning the corner, I saw the house that was burning. I thought it was Alexander's house. As we got closer, everyone stood up on the bus to see. I was sitting next to the window and I heard one of the girls with me say, "That's your mom and dad's house!" At that moment my dream about the burning planes came back to me. I was sitting behind glass, watching huge flames light up the sky.

By the time I stood outside in the crowd, the roof had caved in. There was no way anybody in there could get out. The whole house was on fire. The cops were there.

I was running down the road when somebody said, "Your mom and dad are in there." I said, "No, they're not. They're probably at my granny's house, drinking there." I remember running. And I remember this other girl, whose name is also Ila, running behind me. She was shouting at me to stop running. She finally grabbed my jacket and she threw me down to stop me.

But I got up, ran into my granny's house, and I said, "Where's my mom and dad?" They already knew that the house was on fire. "They're not here," my granny said. "You know where they are. You kids should be at home, looking after your parents, and this wouldn't happen." I ran out of there and back to the burning house. I remember that one of our neighbours grabbed me and took me to their house. I remember going to sleep there and waking up in the middle of the night. Somebody was shouting. I woke up, but I must have gone back to sleep.

When I woke up in the morning, people were singing a hymn in Dene in the next room. They were having a service in the house because it was Christmas Eve. I lay there, listening to the droning voices. The lay reader, John Clipping, was giving a sermon. He said over and over again that alcohol was destroying our people. "Look at what happened last night," he said. "Two people died in a house fire." I knew he was talking about my mom and dad. Gradually, what had happened the night before began to dawn on me. I got up and put on my boots and jacket and walked out through the living room where everyone was singing.

I opened the door. It was still and quiet outside — a strange, beautiful day. Big snowflakes were falling softly. Not a soul anywhere outdoors. It was early morning, and I think a lot of people had been drinking the night before. I looked across the street. There was a big black spot there.

Looking at that black spot, I knew. I knew my mom and dad were dead. I remember standing on the steps for a long time, looking at the charred rubble that used to be my parents' house and crying. Then I began to walk down the road, looking for my brothers and sisters.

I went to Eva Anderson's place, where my brother Horace was staying. When I got there, people were drunk. I went to look for my little sister Marjorie, and everywhere I went there were drunks. My brother Fred came in. "Holy shit," he said. "I thought my mom and dad were gone for sure." He didn't know my mom and dad had died in a house fire the night before. He was drunk. People told him what had happened. He went crazy, began to throw things around. He was never the same for a long time after that.

There was so much drinking, it was as if no one cared. I don't remember much after that, except that I got into the booze too.

On Christmas Eve, I went to a house where the lady was kind and gentle. She offered to wash my clothes, she gave me a change of her clothes while she washed mine. She gave me something to eat. I cried most of that day. As the day went on, people started drinking.

I don't remember much about that day. I must have been offered a drink. I got drunk and blacked out. The next thing I remember is that a guy was raping me. My mind became clear and I tried to get away. He had my neck in a lock and I was unable to move. I started screaming and trying to fight him off but he was too strong.

When I did get away, I scrambled for my clothes that were on the floor and got dressed. I was crying. I ran out the door. It must have been about four or five o'clock in the morning. As soon as I ran out, the wind hit me. The snow was blowing and the wind was howling. My head and my body were aching with pain. I started to run down the road. In the blizzard, I could hardly see where I was going. I wanted to go home. I was longing for my mother. I wanted her to comfort me like she used to when I was very little.

The next thing I remember is that I was lying somewhere and crying. I was calling my mother. "Mom, wait for me. Come back and get me." I had come to die.

Then a woman's voice was telling me to get up, in my language. I said, "No. Leave me alone. I'm going to where my parents are gone." She said, "I can't let you do that." I kept telling her to go away, and she kept pulling on my sleeves. I suddenly realized I was lying on the ashes of our house, at the place where my parents had died the day before. But just before dawn, this woman, who had been one of my mother's friends, pulled me from the rubble of our burnt house. She took me to where my brother was living.

My clothes were all black from the ashes, and I was half frozen. I found my little sister sleeping in one of the rooms and I crawled into bed with her. I didn't bother to take off my jacket or my boots. We held each other and fell asleep crying. This was my Christmas that year. I was seventeen years old.

CAROLINE YASSIE

The night of the fire, my brother Sandy Cheekie was with me at home. We wanted to buy a case of beer, so I called a taxi. The driver said, "Doesn't Sandy Cheekie know that his house is on fire in Dene Village?" I told the cab driver that Sandy Cheekie didn't have a house in the village. He had just come back from South Knife Lake. The driver then said, "Well, anyways, there's a house on fire in Dene Village, whoever's house it is, the last name is Cheekie." I told Sandy what the cab driver had said. I asked him to wait for me. I took that cab to town and went looking for my husband. I found him in the bar and told him what I had just heard. We jumped into his truck and drove full speed to Dene Village. When we got there, the RCMP had blocked the roads going into the village. We got out and ran the rest of the way. By the time we got to the house, there was no way anybody could have escaped. The whole house was engulfed in flames. Everybody was going crazy, yelling and crying. Someone dragged me away from there and took me to the house of an old couple, Charlie and Sophie Sandberry. They locked me inside. They stood against the door and wouldn't let me out. The RCMP ordered all the people to leave the scene except for my husband, Peter Yassie. He helped the RCMP pick up the remains of the bodies.

Later, when he picked me up, we walked past where the house used to be. There was nothing but smoke from the ashes. We got home and I had to break the news to my brother Sandy. When I told him, he didn't believe me, he was in total shock. Then he stayed up all night, crying. The next day was Christmas. I remember my brothers and sisters coming to my house. Everybody was crying. Everything seemed so dark and so cold.

That pain has stayed with me.

ILA BUSSIDOR

I don't remember how long it was before my brothers and sisters could find each other. All I really remember is that when the bus came around to take us to the funeral, it didn't go to St. Paul's Church in town like it usually would. Instead, it took us to the camp at the army base. They took all my brothers and my sisters there.

As we went in, we saw the outline of two coffins draped with a white sheet at the front of the room. I didn't cry, I just felt numb. My brother Fred was sitting there, shaking.

The service started, and my granny Betsy came in, holding this little brown paper bag. I watched her walk up to the front where the coffins were. She took out a tiny wreath of cloth flowers. I noticed they were frayed and faded — and I suddenly realized where they had come from. The only flowers at the funeral, the flowers my granny brought for my mom and dad had come from the garbage dump!

The service was starting, the minister pulled off the white cloth covering the two coffins, and my body went cold. I had imagined my parents would be buried in wooden coffins. But the coffins were gray, just gray metal.

It was a cold, cold day, the snow blowing in our faces. We went to the graveyard by bus and huddled around the hole dug out in the frozen earth. As I watched my parents being buried in their metal coffins, I was thinking, I have to let them go now. From now on, there's nobody to give me direction. No matter how much pain I carry, no matter how much I cry, they're gone. Whatever road I walk in my life, it's all up to me now. No one will guide me. I pushed the aching grief to a place deep in myself.

*

After the tragic death of her parents, Ila Bussidor lost many of the roots that tied her to Dene Village. Over the next few years, she began to drift through life.

ILA BUSSIDOR

After my parents died, I returned to Guelph to the house of Ron and Carole Brooks. I used to cry in the night. Sometimes Carole heard me and came into the room to sleep beside me. She was kind. She and Ron tried to encourage me to hang in there, to finish high school. But I felt out of place. Sometimes I stole their booze to drink with some of the kids I considered friends. Sometimes I hung around downtown instead of going to school.

Ron and Carole wanted me to see the country, to see the world. They paid my way to visit Vancouver. I went and stayed with their friends for a month. They signed me up for a school-organized trip to Europe — to Paris and London. It cost something like $350 for each student. The Brookses paid for me. But the trip was in March, less than three months after my parents' deaths. I was so lonely, I couldn't face it. All I wanted was to be with my sister Marjorie. Instead of going to Europe, I went to Winnipeg to see her.

That summer I went to Churchill with Carole and Ron and stayed with them at Camp. I had a summer job at the hospital again. There, I started drinking a lot. At that time, I didn't think drinking was a problem, I thought it was the most natural thing in the world. Everybody was doing it. I loved to drink.

I couldn't wait for the weekend because it meant going downtown, sitting in the bars all weekend long, going to parties and smoking all the dope I wanted to smoke. I didn't realize that wasn't the way to be. It was the way I had grown up. It was what I saw all around me. The same was true for every single Sayisi Dene person of my generation.

Young girls like me would drink and pass out somewhere. Somebody would come around, some drunk man or some drunk boys, and they would rape us. They took advantage of us as if we were dogs. You'd wake up and find your pants gone. I remember the feeling of shame that would come over me. I didn't want to go out for days. If I knew who that person was, I didn't want him to see me. I would hide until the guilt and the shame gradually wore off, then I would join the other kids again. That's how it was. The whole scene was so ugly that I'm afraid of talking about it.

I tried to commit suicide a couple of times. On my left arm, do you see the scar here? One time we were drunk. I guess I wasn't completely blacked out. I had a glass and I was slashing my wrists. I wanted to die. I was in so much pain. I felt nothing was of any use. My soul was crying and crying. To this day, if I drink, I cry like that. I cry as soon as I drink. Why? Because my spirit is hurt so much. Anyway, I slashed my wrists. There was blood everywhere, all over my clothes. Some girls stopped me. Afterwards, I remember waking up in the morning. My sister was looking for me. They must have heard something. I was sleeping at my friend's place. She said, "Is Ila here?"

Someone said, "Yeah, she's sleeping." So she came into the room where I was sleeping. I woke up and saw my sister by the door. My sister walked over and grabbed my arm. She looked at where I had slashed my wrist. She said, "Gee, this kid is bad." She didn't know why I did that.

Another time, I took a bunch of pills. We were in a house where the woman was taking medication for tuberculosis. There were jars of this medication on the shelf. I got drunk with a bunch of kids. I remember again feeling desperate. I saw all these pills. I don't know how the thought came to my mind. I began to pop these pills — I don't know how many I ate. These kids caught me doing that and they started to force me to throw up. They were shaking me. Throwing me around, saying, "Throw up." I began to puke all this stuff out. All this stuff, yellow and black.

Whenever I attempted suicide, my spirit was crying out for somebody to help me to go on, to become a person — a woman — to live, but who was there to hear me? I was full of grief. It was as if I had already lived a lifetime.

Today, I feel as if during the darkest moments in my life, the spirits of my parents carried me through. They must have saved me from death many times.

After the summer in Churchill, I went back to Guelph with the Brookses, but I was so lonely that I couldn't stay in Guelph anymore. I knew a lot of Dene students were going to school in Winnipeg. I told the Brookses I wanted to go to Winnipeg. At first, they encouraged me to stay and complete the year but I kept saying, "I want to go." I was so unhappy that finally they agreed to help make arrangements through the Department of Indian Affairs. In November, the Brookses found a family in Winnipeg who had once lived in Churchill and with whom I could stay. The man, Dave, worked for the Manitoba Indian Brotherhood.

A lot of kids from Dene Village were living in Winnipeg at that time, so I moved to Winnipeg. I began to go to Sturgeon Creek High School in St. James.

I was very shy. I didn't want to associate with anybody who wasn't Dene because I had known a way of life that was very different from this "nice stuff." These large, warm houses with furniture and appliances, regular meal times, bed times, and social conventions were all alien to me. I knew those things existed, but they had never been a part of my life.

There was this young guy from Pukatawagan who was working with Dave, and I guess Dave must have said, "Why don't you take Ila out? She doesn't go anywhere. She doesn't have any friends." It was arranged that this guy was to take me on a date. I remember I was sitting in the kitchen, reading the newspaper, and he came to talk to me. I didn't look at him, I just kept looking at the paper. I would say yes or no. He asked me if I wanted to go out on a date with him. I thought, What? Holy shit! What's he saying? I said, "No. I can't go." I made up some stupid excuse. He knew I was lying because later on, he asked me again. "Why don't you let me take you to a movie?" he said. He was trying to be nice. I said, "Okay." Dave teased me about it. I thought, I shouldn't have said okay. I should have just said no.

He came to pick me up and he took me to the movie at the Odeon Theatre on Ellice Avenue. I still remember the name of the movie — *The Doctors*, with George C. Scott. He bought popcorn for me. I didn't want to eat the popcorn 'cause I thought he was going to be watching me.

After the movie, he took me downtown. We went to have coffee at this restaurant called Manhattan that I bet you every Native person who went to Winnipeg has been in. It used to be right across from the Bay. We had coffee there and then we got in a cab and he took me all the way home to St. James.

When he walked me to the door, he was going to kiss me goodnight. As soon as he reached for me, I ran in. I felt embarrassed, I felt stupid. I couldn't act normally. There was a wall inside me. I couldn't allow a man to touch me unless I was drunk out of my mind. When I was sober it was impossible.

About a month after that, I got a letter from him. He said he really liked me. He said he knew I was very young and very shy, and he said the next time he came to the city he wanted to take me out again. But two months after that letter he drowned in an accident. He died. My date with him was the first healthy social event in my teen years.

I stayed in school until May that year, but then I dropped out. I never went back regularly after that. I started to drink heavily. I remember being drunk on the streets of Winnipeg. I remember bars on Main Street. I remember I'd be going home on the bus, passing out and being awakened by the cops when the bus had reached the end of the line.

I was lost for a couple of years. I spent my time just wandering around, getting drunk where I could. I had a place to live. I was living with a family who were friends with people I had stayed with before; I helped keep the house clean and took care of their kids in return for a room. To get booze, all I had to do was go downtown and meet friends. We would go to parties and drink. I was brought home by cops many times.

ERNIE BUSSIDOR

I stayed in school through junior high and going on to high school. If you could graduate from grade nine to grade ten, it would be a ticket away from this madness, a ticket out of Churchill. When I finished grade ten, Phil Dickman invited me and a couple of other kids who had finished junior high school to go to Winnipeg and stay at his house. That was how I got out of Dene Village.

I graduated from high school in the summer of '73. Some people had returned to the land, but the majority of our people still lived in Churchill.

I took off to Calgary the day before the graduation because I didn't want to be part of any ceremony. I figured I had put in twelve years of my life to get to where I was, I didn't need a medal from Churchill High School in Winnipeg. In Calgary, I met Phil and his wife and kids again. They were living in Fort Simpson at the time. I went back with them and worked there, doing odd jobs, till September. I returned to Winnipeg in October of '74, and I worked in a paper-box factory for two months while I lived in a little two-room apartment. I was drinking a lot.

RETURN TO THE LAND

Among the adults, there was no hope left. That's something even outsiders sensed and saw. Many of us who grew up in Churchill didn't realize there was a whole history behind how the people had lived before. I saw adults coming to my grand-parents' house with black eyes and scars — they talked about somebody's death. But mostly they talked about how to get alcohol. (Ernie Bussidor)

Dene Village had been a disaster almost from the day it was established. The bureaucrats who planned the settlement had repeated most of the mistakes made with Camp-10. They had chosen an unsuitable piece of land on poorly drained muskeg. They had built houses that were wrong for the people and wrong for the sub-arctic climate, they had placed them close together, and they had seg-regated the Dene. They had ignored the deep social, psychological, and spiritual wounds that were destroying the people.

In Dene Village, family breakdown and social disintegration had accelerated. The Dene, who made up five percent of Churchill's population, accounted for seventy-five percent of the police activity; their children, who made up ten percent of the school enrollment, constituted almost all the truancy.[1]

After only a couple of years in Dene Village, the people felt doomed. Elders occasionally talked among themselves about their lives before the relocation. They even wondered about getting out of "this hell" and returning to their earlier life, but their spirits were so broken that they didn't know where they would go or how. Thirteen years after the relocation from Duck Lake to Camp-10, many of the people who had been adults in 1956 had died. Only a handful of the adults in Dene Village were sober at any given time.

Most people associated with the non-Aboriginal institutions in Churchill — the town, the government, the school, the police, and even the church — blamed the Sayisi Dene for their own suffering. They blamed the adults for drinking, for not keeping jobs, and for neglecting their children.[2] The few outsiders who were sympathetic to the Dene were bewildered by the atrocities in the settlement and felt powerless in the face of such severe social and spiritual decay.

In 1968, the Manitoba Department of Health and Social Services hired Phil Dickman as Community Development Officer; his job was to help the Dene adjust to life in Dene Village. In 1969, Dickman wrote an article entitled "Thoughts on Relocation" for a magazine called *The Musk-Ox*, analyzing the forces destroying the Dene. In it, he says:

> The best example that can be given of the unbelievable tragedy that results from centralized bureaucratic decision-making when combined with ignorance of the will of the people is to be found in Dene Village. Every decision that has been made, beginning with the move from Duck Lake and ending with the construction and design of the houses, has been based on two false premises: the first, that outside experts know better than the people; and the second, that a political structure created by government, the band council, expresses the will of the people.
>
> Today, the people live in a village which they believe they did not choose, and live in houses for which they did not originally ask. Neither was requested by the people and so they believe that they carry no responsibility for their plight.[3]

In the same article, Dickman suggests an alternative to life in Dene Village:

> Beginning with the adults, mostly over thirty years old, who have no chance of adapting to urban life, an opportunity must be provided them of returning to the fishing, hunting and trapping for which they were trained and in which they have long experience. By direct intervention of government their way of life was taken away. It is now government's obligation to find the means whereby they can be restored to productive and useful living as judged by their own standards. If the people want it, government must enable them to follow the old ways in their own land as long as they live. For this group, settlement in productive areas of the Chipewyan land for at least part of each year seems the best solution.[4]

The longer Dickman worked with the people, the more he believed that a return to the land might restore the independence of the Sayisi Dene: "When I learned where the people in Dene Village had come from, I began to wonder if there was a way they could go back. From the way people like Chief Simon Duck talked about their life before Churchill, I knew they had a longing for the land. All I did was bring that longing out in the open. It seemed to me that it could break the cycle of drunkenness and misery. I raised the subject with the chief and council. They first said they had no money, no means."[5]

Meanwhile, the federal government had unfinished business with the Sayisi Dene. Treaty Five, which was signed in August 1910, had promised band members 160 acres per family of five as reserve land. That land entitlement had never been settled. The land around Duck Lake would no longer be suitable for a reserve because the former trading post had been sold to the provincial Game Branch for one dollar as a field station. Before the relocation from Duck Lake to Camp-10, the Dene had sometimes camped and fished on the shores of South Knife and North Knife Lakes, about 160 kilometres west of Churchill and eighty kilometres south of Duck Lake. Now, Dickman encouraged band members to explore that land and use it.

If a small group could live near North Knife Lake for a year, hunting, trapping and fishing, others could also consider a return to a life of purpose and competence. In 1969, Dickman approached the Indian Agent, Bud Schroder, with the idea. He found Schroeder sympathetic:

> The Indian Agent had an inkling of how wrong everything was for the Sayisi Dene in Churchill. He wanted to get that trip to North Knife Lake to happen. He secured a little bit of money. Already at that time, the chief and the band council were beginning to see that the best way to get some money for this was to get it out of the band's allocation. We were looking for a thousand dollars there, a hundred dollars here, to try to put together enough for a bunch of people to go off to North Knife Lake.[6]

The dream was sweet. But for people drowning in alcohol, an experiment in returning to the land was an enormous challenge. In the thirteen years since the relocation from Duck Lake to Camp-10, one-third of the community's population had died, and knowledge of valuable survival skills had been lost with them. Leadership was problematic. In *The Musk-Ox*, Phil Dickman writes:

> Outside of the religious, political and economic structures imposed on them by white society, there is little, if any organized leadership in the community; . . . there is an endemic fear of any leadership that is not created and maintained by the white man. And that fear seems to be strongest within the person with ability who innately wants to do something for himself and his people. "Leave me alone, I'll do it myself" and "I don't want to get involved" are the all too frequent defensive replies to requests for leadership action.[7]

To begin to explore a return to the land, the people needed someone who knew the land well and who still had the traditional skills. No one in Dene Village was up to the task. Finally, someone remembered that a man named Ronnie John Bussidor had stayed near North River and continued to live off the land with his wife and her parents. Ronnie John was fifty years old at the time. He remembers the day when Phil Dickman approached him:

> We used to visit Dene Village once in a while, to drink with the people. There was so much noise in that place that it was like the yelling you hear at a hockey game. In 1969, while I continued to live across the river, I got a message that a white man was interested in talking to me. I had no idea who it was or what he wanted.
>
> My wife and I went across to the mainland on a boat. When we got to Churchill, we saw a truck parked on the road. A man came out of the truck, approached me and introduced himself as Phil Dickman. "I want to talk to you," he said. Peter Yassie was sitting in the truck.
>
> Phil Dickman said, "I want to talk to you about a plan we have to move people back to the land, to the traditional territory." He wanted me to help with this plan because I knew the land.
>
> "If this is what you want to talk about," I said, "this involves people's lives. Men like us don't talk about this kind of thing standing on the road. If you are serious, set up a meeting with the people and I'll be there."
>
> After this brief conversation, I forgot about it. In spring when I was in Churchill, this man, Phil Dickman, approached me again, and again in August, after he had set up a meeting. "In September you can start on this journey," he said to me. He wanted me to scout out the land, to check the fishing and the hunting before other people would set out. I said, "I will go only if my wife comes with me. But we can't go all alone, you have to pick five other people to go with us."

Dickman soon found five more people willing to go with Ronnie John Bussidor and his wife, Mary, to check out the land around North Knife River and to try living there. The volunteers were George and Mary Sandberry, Charlie Ellis, Sandy Clipping, and Charlie Thomas. They began to hold meetings to discuss and plan their project. They would take their supplies to South Knife Lake by boat on the South Knife River, and from there they would proceed on foot overland the next forty-eight kilometres to North Knife Lake. They needed boats, motors, traps, and clothes.

Only one person in Dene Village was fully employed at the time: Peter Yassie. Bud Schroeder, the Indian Agent, asked Peter to work with the group. Peter's widow, Caroline, remembers that, at first, her husband refused:

> Peter was working with Pan American Airways, he wanted to mind his own business. But they kept coming to him. He thought about the request and about his relatives in Dene Village, and how the people were suffering. He wanted to help the people. In the end, he accepted the job Indian Affairs was offering him.

He then started to talk to the people in Dene Village about moving back to our homeland. He wanted the people to make this decision themselves. He found it very hard to do this because there was a lot of drinking going on. But he managed to get enough people interested.

When Peter Yassie accepted the job, he became the first Dene to be hired full time by the Department of Indian Affairs.

The last supplies arrived late in September, and the group set out from Churchill on September 25, with seven boats with outboard motors. Peter Yassie joined them with his own boat and motor. Phil Dickman and two other government employees, John Hickes and Celestine Thorassie, would go along for some of the way to help with the journey.

The trip was very hard. We had to travel by boat up the river on the barren land. We had to drag our boats on sleds. One evening the group was running out of food supplies so the men had to go hunting. They shot some geese and that was our food for the rest of this trip. We had to cross major rapids. Our lives were in danger all the way.

The boats had to be dragged across the rapids. After we crossed all the rapids the trip became a little easier. The men shot a moose and the women got together and cut up all the meat. We made dry meat to carry with us. Before sunrise, all the meat was prepared and the moose hide was scraped and packed. We didn't waste any part of the meat.

At South Knife Lake, our little group had to set up tents and start a little community. We had very few tools to work with and not a lot of food, but I remember the joy of the people who were on that trip. We were all sober. We got our strength back and, most important of all, we felt we still had the skills to survive on the land. (Caroline Yassie)

During that trip, Phil Dickman caught a glimpse of the lost ways of the Sayisi Dene:

One day, we saw a moose standing on a sandy point near the shore. One of the men shot it. The people in the group skinned it and cut it up right there. I was astounded at their skill at butchering, and at keeping the meat clean. It was a revelation to me. One evening, we stopped at a lovely place full of jack pines on the edge of the river. It was late, we were tired, and this was like park land. We unloaded the boats to camp for the night. Three of us walked a little inland and found some mounds. The Dene knew immediately that this was a burial ground where people who died in a smallpox epidemic in the nineteenth century were buried. Even though it was dark and we had already set up camp, they decided to leave. They started to pack up right away. They wouldn't stay there because of the spirits. This was revealing to me. I understood how they must have suffered when they were forced to live in Camp-10.[8]

Ronnie John Bussidor's knowledge of the land helped the group make its way:

> It took us fifteen and a half days to reach South Knife Lake. I was always going ahead of the group, there were a lot of rapids you had to watch for. For half of the way we were helped by a white man, Phil Dickman. Up to South Knife Lake, Peter Yassie, John Hickes and Celestine Thorassie were with us. There they left. From there on, we had to walk. We waited for freeze-up, and then we set out on foot, pulling the sleds with the supplies. We got to North Knife Lake on November 3, 1969. We lived there for two years.

At Christmas, one of the people who trekked to North Knife Lake, Mary Sandberry, returned to Churchill because she was sick. She told the Sayisi Dene at Churchill that the people who had returned to the land had enough to eat, they had been trapping for some furs, and they were happy to be there. They had started to play the drum again and to sing the songs of the northern wilderness.

By spring it was apparent that the spirits and the physical health of all seven who went to North Knife Lake had vastly improved and that they were happy to remain there. Phil Dickman, who visited them, was delighted: "I remember a couple at North Knife Lake living in a tiny old trapper's cabin. I went inside. Here they were living in a mud cabin, and it was so tidy, clean and sweet smelling that I was astounded. The floor was covered thick with spruce boughs. This was a clean environment and they were happy. They were in their element."

In 1971, more families decided to move away from Churchill and return to the land. The next winter (1971-72), twenty people were living at North Knife Lake, a couple of families tried out South Knife Lake, and all of them were able to fish and trap with support and supplies from the Department of Indian Affairs. A dream was coming true, the movement to return to the land was gaining momentum. But North Knife and South Knife Lakes could not sustain this growing community. "North Knife Lake isn't really solid land. When the rest of the community in Dene Village decided they would return to the land, we realized there wasn't enough caribou around North Knife Lake to sustain everyone. We began to look for a more suitable location" (John Solomon).

The officials of the Department of Indian Affairs were eager to establish a settlement at South Knife Lake and get it over with. At a band meeting at South Knife Lake, they said, "We can't move you anymore." But the next day, the band members held their own meeting and decided that they would move themselves.

This was a turning point. That summer, the chief of the band was Alex Sandberry, and with the support of his people, he took a stand against the officials of the

Department of Indian Affairs. On June 28, 1971, in a letter to the Manitoba regional director of Indian Affairs, Sandberry wrote:

> We are not children, and we, the same as the white man will use resource people in a manner we feel will be the most beneficial to us and our people the same as you use a lawyer, doctor, economic consultant, engineer etc. If you insist on defending your staff, right or wrong, then you cannot be accepting in practice the principle of assisting us toward the goal of attaining self government but are rather helping perpetuate control of our people by your staff.[9]

The Sayisi Dene were taking control of their lives:

> The people weren't satisfied with the land around South and North Knife Lake. There was no caribou, not enough fish. The people wanted to move again. They had to look for another spot.
>
> Peter Yassie contacted me from Churchill through a two-way radio. He took a plane to come and get me so we could scout for another area — we would look at Tadoule Lake. I was the only one who had a Skidoo. We put it on the plane. The plane landed at the north end of Tadoule Lake, where the Seal River flows towards Churchill. John Mackenzie, the Indian agent in Churchill, was also there. Peter Yassie, Fred Duck, and I went all over the shore, checking out the land. (Ronnie John Bussidor)

Jimmy Clipping was in the first group that set out to check the land around Tadoule Lake:

> It took us thirteen days before we hit the lake — we hit Tadoule Lake from South Knife Lake. We travelled mostly in the evenings and early part of the morning. We would have a few hours of sleep during the night. Sometimes we didn't even sleep. We stayed up all night. If we travelled during the day when it was thawing out and the sun was out we were just bogging in and we couldn't move, so we slept during the day and travelled during the night when the snow was hard to travel on. The dogs would stay on top of the snow. We tried with our snowshoes to break trails, but we broke our snowshoes, they were soaking wet, there was never a night that I went to bed with dry clothes because I was soaking wet right up to my arms, right up to my chest every day. The snow was deep and it was hard travelling so the only alternative we had was to camp for the day. . . .
>
> Just before we got to Tadoule Lake we hit Shetane Lake and we ran into some caribou there, the caribou were still migrating north at that time. So we ran into some caribou there and we killed some and we spent two days drawing, getting the water out of it; it would be less weight for the dogs to carry. We spent two days in Shetane on the west side of the lake and then we travelled up the lake to MeGassa, and in MeGassa we spent another night; then from MeGassa next morning we hit Tadoule Lake.

Their ancestors had called that lake *Ts'eouli* (floating ashes). Fish were plentiful in its clear waters. The land surrounding it was made up of large sand deposits from glaciers that had melted thousands of years ago. Sandy eskers on both sides of the lake resembled the traditional camp grounds of the Sayisi Dene. Forests of jack pine, birch, and black spruce gave shelter to herds of moose. Everyone felt this could be home:

It's just like we hit a paradise here, and about two days later, Indian Affairs landed here and they said to us, "You people said you were going to move, it looks like you meant it." And we told them, "Yes, we do, and if you still don't want to move us we will go back and pick up the rest of the families and we'll tell them we have located a place." . . . Then they said, "Okay, looks like you guys meant it so we'll help you out." The following week, they said, "Next week, we'll bring down your families," so that's when the original move began. The following week a DC-3 came in here with our families, and we started building homes. Before that, we looked all the way around Tadoule Lake and to the south of Tadoule Lake there was a big esker there, which we now call the summer camp. Summer camp, meaning that that's the first summer that we spent in Tadoule Lake. (Jimmy Clipping)

John Solomon remembers: "Peter Yassie helped a great deal in this move. He said he would try to get us to the point where we would just have to flick on the lights and turn on televisions if we want. This he did accomplish eventually."

In May 1973, the Sayisi Dene who were still at Dene Village began to abandon it and settle on the north shore of Tadoule Lake. That summer, they set up tents scattered widely among the birch, pine, and spruce on a high esker bluff overlooking the lake. Each morning, their nets were full of trout, pike, and pickerel. It was as if they had awakened from a nightmare. The band unanimously decided to ban alcohol from the community.

In the winter of 1973, the people at Tadoule Lake built twenty-eight new log cabins to house the seventy-five adults and twelve pre-school children. School-aged children belonging to the families were at schools in Winnipeg, Dauphin, and Brandon.[10]

Peter Yassie had played an important role in the Sayisi Dene's return to the land. During the first couple of years after the new community was established at Tadoule Lake, he continued to work as the community development officer for the Department of Indian Affairs. In 1975, the band members elected him chief. He had been one of the most successful members of the band. He had always been employed, and he had earned a commercial pilot's licence and even owned a small plane. He had successfully lobbied the federal government for funds to build an airstrip at Tadoule Lake. He had installed a generator in the community, fulfilling his promise to light the houses at the flick of a switch.

But, like everyone else in Tadoule Lake, he struggled with the demons of alcoholism and family violence that had taken hold in Camp-10 and Dene Village. Churchill had claimed the lives of four of his six children: three had died in a house fire, and a fourth, a baby, had died of pneumonia. And he and his wife, Caroline, suffered yet another terrible blow. In 1987, their adult son Howard, who had joined the RCMP, shot himself to death at the deserted site of Dene Village. A few years later, in his early fifties, Peter Yassie himself died from a heart attack.

ILA BUSSIDOR

In 1974, I was at Tadoule Lake for the first time. I was nineteen. I was living in Winnipeg at the time and going to school. The people had just settled at Tadoule. During summer holidays I had returned to Churchill and found Dene Village abandoned. A group of people, including my sister Sarah and Peter Yassie, Peter Thorassie, and a couple of guys from the Department of Indian Affairs were going to Tadoule Lake for Treaty Days. I decided to get on the plane with them, a small, single-engine Beaver.

It was a bright summer day. The plane landed by this huge sand beach. There were a lot of people on the beach. We walked up to them and shook hands with some people. That felt weird because shaking hands — greeting people — wasn't something I was accustomed to doing.

The big, blue lake was so beautiful that I was speechless. I had never seen or dreamt of anything so beautiful. The air smelt fresh, clean. There were trees everywhere — birch and black spruce all the way up to the esker. Tents were scattered between them. Perhaps deep inside, I recognized this was the way my people used to live a long time ago.

The strangest and the most touching thing that day was that every single person on that beach was stone sober! That was the most striking difference between Tadoule Lake and Dene Village. It was a new world — clean and spacious. I was blown away.

I walked up to my sister Caroline's tent. It had a wooden frame around it. Inside, there was a little stove in a corner, a couple of beds, a little table, and a pail of water. Everything was clean and tidy.

I wasn't there to stay. The group I was with would fly out again later that day. I left with them. But I knew I wanted to come back.

The next time I came to Tadoule, it was in winter. By then, the people had started to build log cabins. My sister Caroline had a brand new cabin. Smoke was coming out of the chimneys. There were wood piles beside people's doors. When you walked into somebody's house, you didn't knock, you just walked in. You sat down, had a cup of tea.

The people were busy, everybody was working. You could feel the hope and the sense of purpose in the air. They were building something. People were hunting, too. There was caribou meat. My sister fried some and I ate lots. I hadn't eaten caribou meat for so many years and I ate so much that I remember getting sick from it.

I remember some people had dog-teams. That's something I remembered from my early childhood, but I hadn't seen it in all the years in Churchill. Something else I had never seen in Churchill was a Skidoo. A couple of people in Tadoule Lake had Skidoos at that time.

I remember the hole in the ice on the lake. People carried water home in pails. There was no TV. Some people had little transistor radios — that was their only connection with the outside world. That isolation was what made the settlement so special. That solitude in the silence of the wilderness was something the people needed. It felt like a time for people to start to heal. It was a totally new way of life, and I wanted to be a part of it.

But I didn't know how to live this kind of life. If I was asked to go get wood, I didn't know what was dry wood and what was green wood. I didn't know how to make a hole in the ice. I didn't know how to dry meat. I didn't know how to prepare any kind of meat to keep it for a long time. I didn't know how to fish. The young men were in a similar situation. They didn't know how to hunt, how to set out fish nets.

When you live in a place like Tadoule Lake, you have to know those things to survive. You have to know how to make a fire. But so many people were dead, and the surviving elders were so damaged that there was no one to teach us how to do those things. The skills that were handed down through the generations were the skills of survival and independence. Soon we realized that they were lost.

So was our language. Lost. In Churchill we had learned English and lost Dene. The surviving elders spoke only Dene — which meant a tremendous problem of communication in the community.

The burst of energy and hope of building a new life in Tadoule Lake gradually gave way to discouragement and a sense of loss as we began to face the difficulties. As time went on, we also began to see that the wounds people had received in Churchill were festering and spreading, and that, unless we began to heal those wounds, they would reach out into the future, injuring our children and crippling future generations.

MARY YASSIE

I first came to Tadoule Lake from Churchill in August 1976. When we got off the plane I couldn't believe how beautiful it was, the sand beach and all these trees everywhere, and all the sober people who greeted us. I was happy that we got out of Churchill to start a new life here in the wilderness, and at the same time I was afraid that I might not survive this way of life, as I had no skills to live off the land. I used to cry, out of relief and fear of the unknown. After a while I got used to this different way. My husband built a log cabin and slowly we started to rebuild our lives away from alcohol. Our lives seemed so peaceful, we were young and we had a chance to raise a family here.

ERNIE BUSSIDOR

By December 1974, there were hardly any Sayisi Dene left in Dene Village. The houses were still standing but they were empty. Eventually they were dismantled. The townspeople built cottages with the materials up along Goose Creek.

That winter, I came to Tadoule Lake for the first time. The community was about a year and a half old. My grandparents and my uncle were living in a little two-room cabin. I lived with them for about a month.

The people were trying to live by trapping and hunting once again. Once a month they got some groceries from Churchill. They had made an agreement with the welfare office — they would phone in their orders to the S & M store in Churchill, and their welfare vouchers would be processed in Churchill to pay for their orders and they would get their box of groceries by plane.

There were about eight snowmobiles in the community: Elans. Some people had transistor radios. Everybody lived in log cabins. There was caribou. No hydro, no band hall, no school, nothing. It was so quiet. Oh man, it was paradise!

But I was restless. I returned to Churchill after a month. I got a job at the construction site of the recreation complex. They wouldn't hire any Dene, so I lied. I said I was from Winnipeg. I don't look Dene anyway. They hired me. I worked for four months, long enough to buy a snowmobile — an Arctic Cat — for about $1,000. I brought it back to Tadoule Lake.

It was a hopeful time. But as the community emerged, so did our demons. When people of my generation began to have families, we realized we didn't know how to live in peace with ourselves and our partners. People would suppress their demons with alcohol and with drugs whenever they could.

If we could heal, we could stop the circle of destruction so that our kids wouldn't grow up to be like me. The way I grew up. I still have a lot of demons in me that I'm trying to conquer. It's hard, but I try every day.

*

In the summer of 1976, as the new community of Tadoule Lake was taking shape, love took Ila Cheekie and Ernie Bussidor by surprise.

ERNIE BUSSIDOR

I was messed up emotionally. I had never had a father figure to base anything on in life. I had no emotional connection with anybody. And then Ila came into my life.

I knew who she was. We had grown up together, but we stumbled into each other in 1977 as young adults in Tadoule Lake. Holy smokes! I knew this woman was something else. I was totally smitten by her shyness and her innocence. I started visiting her. We spent more and more time together.

I knew I was getting myself into something very scary because I had never loved anybody, I had never been loved. I knew this woman was important.

One day I pitched up a tent, and one night at three a.m. we took our two cups and our two blankets, our two plates, two forks, and moved in together.

I realized right away that it was going to be very tough to try to connect on an emotional level. That was something very foreign to me. I began to treat her the way I saw my uncle and other people around me when I was a kid treat their partners. I couldn't help it — I didn't know any other way. I was possessive and insecure.

Soon we began to fight. We fought, oh man. We went through a lot of angry words. Real hurting words. Rough periods. We didn't know what was happening to us. I built a little cabin for us in 1978. But we were fighting. Then it got even rougher, we got into physical violence.

Then Jason was born. We both wanted to go to school, so we came to Winnipeg. There, alcohol became a force in our lives again. Our relationship became more and more violent. I would drink and then I would hit her and then I would sober up and I would be remorseful. It was a cycle. She would forgive me, we would go through a honeymoon phase. But our honeymoon phases became shorter and shorter. The terrible thing was that I knew something was very wrong — but I had no idea what it was, or why. It was as if some other force would get ahold of us — that's the only way I can describe it.

I'm so sorry for Jason because he grew up in an environment where I was totally unable to understand what was wrong. I knew we had problems, we knew we both had short fuses but we couldn't figure out why.

Ila and I are important to each other. We understand each other a lot of the time but I guess we have similar wounds.

I realize that alcohol is very destructive for our people. I know that many people who were our caregivers when we were little didn't even make it to my age — thirty-nine — because of alcohol. You could see the change that came upon them when they drank. We saw when we were young how extreme people's behaviour became from alcohol.

When I am stressed out, when something is bothering me, I tend to drink to relieve that stress. I have a weakness with alcohol. At least once a year, I get into an embarrassing situation because of alcohol. My outbursts with Ila often happen when I drink. When you are involved in band affairs as I am, you have nothing to hide behind when you get into embarrassing situations because of alcohol. I am working on facing my demons. Ila is adamant against alcohol, and she is right.

We are trying to break the cycle. In 1993, Ila, our children, and I spent four weeks at an Aboriginal healing centre in Alberta: the Poundmaker's Lodge. It helped. I was forced to deal with myself. But healing doesn't happen just once. We have to heal again and again. We have gone to family therapy for a few months. That helped too.

I would say Ila and I get along better now. When we age together, I hope we will settle down and be close to each other. If you're willing to stick it out that long, you can work things out in the end.

ILA BUSSIDOR

I knew Ernie all my life — we had grown up in Dene Village together, and we had gone to high school together. When I met him in Tadoule Lake around 1976, we started to live together. I didn't really have anywhere else to go. Most of my brothers and sisters were living at Tadoule Lake already, but they had their own families.

Ernie and I grew really attached to each other. We were young and in love. I wanted to build my life around him. I am sure he felt the same way about me. Ernie was the first person to whom I was close enough to say that I had been raped. For a long time, he was the only one who knew.

When I was a kid in Dene Village, I used to see my sisters and other women beaten and it showed on their faces. I used to see people getting beaten on the street too. I used to think that was just the way it was supposed to be. If you get married, your husband could punch you out and it was part of your marriage. Isn't that crazy? That's what we saw. That's what we lived.

I think one of the first things I noticed even before we started living together was the jealousy. When we started to live together it increased. That's when the physical violence started.

In 1978 we had our first baby: Jason. As soon as Ernie and I became parents, exactly what I hadn't wanted for my babies started to happen. Ernie and I had survived Dene Village, but we were carrying the disease. The destruction we had seen while we were growing up had affected us as if someone had injected us with poison. The disease was not as visible as it had been in Dene Village, there wasn't as much noise. But the hell we had lived through was starting again in a different way.

Ernie and I both wanted to go back to school so we applied to the Red River Community College in Winnipeg, and we were accepted. The three of us moved to Winnipeg. That was a very difficult year for me. That year, my little sister Marjorie died of tubercular meningitis. She was a year younger than me and one of the most beautiful people I have known.

Marjorie died in October. I returned to Tadoule Lake for her funeral. The lake was freezing up. In those days, there was no airport, no runway, just a lake. I remember that this time the plane had to land on the esker. It couldn't land on the lake until it was completely frozen.

I had brought my baby, Jason, with me, and the little daughter of my sister who had died. Sheila was five years old.

There were a lot of things I couldn't handle at that time. I had to learn to deal with my sister's death, and I had to deal with what was happening to Ernie and me.

We were drinking a lot. Ernie had started to beat me. I remember one time he beat me up really bad. My ears were swollen. My ear drums were broken. I went to the Health Sciences Centre to take a hearing test. Ernie came with me. An Oriental doctor took me into a room and checked me out. He had seen other scars, in my other ear, where my ear drums had been broken before many times from getting slapped or hit. I remember that doctor asking, "Did he do it?" I said, "No." I was protecting Ernie.

It was always like that. A lot of times, I would be taken into the hospital with, say, a gall bladder problem after I drank. I would be rushed to the emergency. They would have to undress me — and there were all these bruises all over my body. Great big bruises on my arms, blue wherever I was hit.

They would ask me what those bruises were. I would lie: "I went roller skating. I had an accident." I was continuously hiding the truth. These people at the hospital knew I was lying.

I remember times when I went from bar to bar in Thompson, looking for Ernie even though I had a black eye from a fight with him. I never considered leaving him. I couldn't imagine living without him. I had to have him with me. I thought if he left me, I wouldn't be able to live.

It's a cycle. We go for a while without violence, and then it erupts. I have too much hurt and bitterness in me. I throw that all at him and he can't take it. That's when the verbal violence starts. I say things to really hurt him because I can't hurt him physically — he is stronger than me. That's when I bring it out in him. He has to hurt me back so he starts hitting me.

After that year in Winnipeg, we returned to Tadoule Lake, and I started to work for the band as a clerk in the store. Next, I worked as band administrator. I think that's where I learned what was going on between the band and the Department of Indian Affairs. That's when I began to understand what had happened to our people when the relocation had taken place. I began to get interested in politics.

Just about everyone at Tadoule Lake suffers from similar cycles. You can feel the pain that my generation of people lives with. It's something you just can't get rid of easily. It comes out in violence, in drinking, drugging, hurting other people.

The heartbreaking thing about all this is that we find ourselves re-living all the horrors we've longed to get away from. I was determined to protect my children, to give them a good life. I am struggling for that. It's something people don't want to talk about, but we have to talk about it in order to begin to heal.

Healing doesn't happen all at once. It happens in steps. I believe I've started to take some steps. I can't change anyone else, but I have the power to change myself, and I believe I made some good choices. I choose not to drink, most of the time. I know that drinking can be the most destructive thing I can do. If you drink and you get into a fight, you can get killed or you can kill somebody. I don't want that kind of chaos to be part of my life any more. I made a decision not to abuse alcohol the way I had seen it abused at Camp-10 and Dene Village. It has made a big difference. But I still struggle with it. If I had kept drinking the way people at Dene Village had, maybe I wouldn't be alive today. Maybe Ernie would be in jail. As a sober person, I have the strength to recognize a lot of things and to try to make some corrections.

When we were younger, when Ernie made a jealous comment, I would automatically get upset, and the fight would escalate. Now, I can let it go. Sometimes I even laugh — and the argument fizzles away. Slowly, our relationship is getting healthier.

TADOULE LAKE

On the map of northern Manitoba, the lake known to the Dene as *Ts'eouli* is marked as Tadoule Lake. Elders tell two different stories about why their ancestors called this lake *Ts'eouli* (floating ashes). According to the first story, the Dene who camped near the lake in the eighteenth century, during the Cree-Dene wars, used to put the ashes of their campfires in the lake to avoid smoke. "Whatever you throw in this lake, it swirls around for months," they say. "Those ashes swirling in the water must have given the lake its name."

The second story describes how, a long time ago, a forest fire forced a group of Dene who were making birch-bark canoes along the shore to leave their teepees and rush to the water to save their lives while the wind blew ashes towards the lake. Later, when they returned to their campsite, they discovered something amazing: the fire had burnt all the trees and all the grass but had left their tents untouched.

These old stories confirm what the Sayisi Dene already know: that this settlement is in their ancient territory. Band members were glad when it received reserve status. But their land entitlement remained unsettled. That meant that the people didn't know exactly how large a piece of land they could call their own and, without that information, they couldn't make plans for economic development. The Sayisi Dene had unfinished business with the Government of Canada.

And there was more to the unfinished business than land entitlement. The Sayisi Dene also wanted public acknowledgement, a recognition of the wrong that was done to them. They wanted an apology from the Government of Canada. When Ila Bussidor became chief in 1988, one of her highest priorities was to tell Canadians about the relocation of her people and the effect it had had on them.

By the time the Royal Commission on Aboriginal Peoples was established and had begun to hold public hearings, Ila was no longer chief, but she continued to speak out. On June 1, 1993, she appeared before the Commission's public hearing in Thompson and requested that the commissioners hold a special consultation at Tadoule Lake. Her message to the Commission was direct:

> My people were moved by the federal government from Little Duck Lake to Churchill in 1956. This relocation destroyed our independence and ruined our way of life. After fifteen years of neglect and despair in Churchill, we could begin to count the dead. More than 100 of my people, one-third of our population, died in the Churchill Camps because of this unplanned, misdirected government action. This didn't happen a thousand miles from here, or a hundred years ago; . . . it happened to my people, my family, thirty to thirty-five years ago. It seems like only yesterday, and it affects us still today.[1]

They accepted. In early October 1993, the commissioners arrived at Tadoule Lake to hear submissions, to hold public meetings, and to conduct interviews. Three years later, when the Commission released its five-volume report, it publicly and officially acknowledged the injustice that was done to the Sayisi Dene. Their years of humiliation and pain in Churchill were now on record.

> The story of the 1956 relocation of the Sayisi Dene of northern Manitoba is both tragic and complex. It is another example of government officials operating with no specific relocation policy, attempting to find solutions to a number of perceived problems. Their actions were taken, however, with little understanding of the effects they might have. . . . We heard many stories about the destructive effects of this relocation, about the suffering of people torn from their homeland, and about their feeling of powerlessness to stop what was happening to them.[2]

In 1989, the Sayisi Dene First Nation at Tadoule Lake joined nineteen other Manitoba bands who had outstanding land entitlement and formed the Treaty Land Entitlement Committee to bargain collectively with the federal and provincial governments. In May 1996, they signed a tentative agreement that granted the Sayisi Dene First Nation 23,000 acres of land (about 9,000 hectares) and $580,000 for economic development.

Just before the Sayisi Dene had started their land entitlement negotiations, the federal government had signed with the Inuit a comprehensive land claims deal called Nunavut. Nunavut gave 12,950 hectares of traditional Dene territory to the Inuit. Elders like John Solomon were outraged: "Each year, our ancestors took their children, their families, and crossed three rivers in canoes made of caribou skins, to get to the barren lands beyond Tha-anne Yetthe (South Henick Lake) and Edehon Lake. We can't let those lands go."

The Royal Commission on Aboriginal Peoples also acknowledged the Sayisi Dene's continuing struggle to have their rights to their homeland recognized: "The fact that their traditional lands have been included within the boundaries of Nunavut adds to the Sayisi Dene's sense of grievance and, they believe, is another example of how their interests have been ignored by the federal government."[3]

In March 1993, the band went to court to challenge Nunavut. They asserted that they had treaty rights north of the sixtieth parallel (the southern boundary of Nunavut). Shortly after that, the Inuit agreed to "freeze" 42,030 hectares (106,000 acres) of land within Nunavut (the amount of unfulfilled treaty land entitlement claimed by the Sayisi Dene) pending the trial.

In 1996, the settlement on the north shore of Tadoule Lake was twenty-three years old. It represented the survival of the Sayisi Dene to face the twenty-first century — a triumph of their spirit. As elder John Solomon put it, "The Dene are a hardy people to have suffered so much and to continue their travels."

Daily scheduled flights into and out of Tadoule Lake land on an airstrip a couple of kilometres to the north of the settlement. In winter, snowmobiles gather behind a wire fence surrounding the airstrip. Men unload boxes of groceries and household goods from the planes and load them onto the snowmobiles. Behind the airport, a Manitoba Hydro diesel generator hums day and night to provide electricity for the community. Piles of wood are stacked beside all the houses scattered near the shore and up on the esker. Low afternoon sun shines on windows — none of them broken — and on plastic stretched over window frames for insulation. Snowmobiles whizz up and down snow-covered slopes. To the northwest of the community, at the highest point of land, a new circular building with large windows rises among tall black spruce and tamarack: the brand new Peter Yassie Memorial School, which opened in September 1995 and which accommodates 112 students from kindergarten to grade twelve. The school, owned and administered by the band, has become a symbol of hope and regeneration for the people of Tadoule Lake, a resource centre for the entire community.

Each night, the school offers activities to people in different age groups. Tuesday nights, teenagers play basketball, volleyball, and floor hockey in the gym. Wednesday night is women's night, with aerobics classes and volleyball games. The highlight of the week is Friday — gym night for young children. The kids play floor hockey and Red Rover under the supervision of the physical education teacher, while parents socialize with each other. The school bus goes around the community picking people up and dropping them off.

During recess every day, children — all dressed in colourful snow suits or ski jackets, all wearing mitts, hats, and snow boots — shout and laugh on monkey bars and slides in the playground in front of the school. Teenagers play road hockey on the large skating rink behind the school. Ila and Ernie Bussidor's eighteen-year-old son, Jason, is among them. Kids like Jason no longer have to leave their families to go to high school.

At noon, the children go home for lunch. None of them returns hungry. Most food is flown in from the south, and it's expensive. People probably eat too much fatty food like chips and cheezies and not enough fresh fruits and vegetables. But most cupboards are stocked.

Ila tends to stock too much food. "Ernie tells me it's a waste. I know he is right, but I have to have a lot of food in the house," she says. "If I ever saw Rosie and Dennis hungry like I was as a little girl, I wouldn't want to live. As long as I am alive, they won't go hungry, whatever it takes."

Some people occasionally hunt moose or geese and catch fish. And every fall, the band council organizes a caribou harvest. It charters a plane to take a group of hunters out to the barren lands; it's an expensive ritual, but cherished as a remnant of the past. Caribou remain special to everyone at Tadoule Lake, even to the children who have no idea what it once meant to their ancestors.

Since snowmobiles have replaced snowshoes, and since gas is extremely expensive, trapping has become an occasional pastime. Elders like Charlie Kithithee and Thomas Duck, who still trap, do it more for old times' sake than to make a living.

As the twentieth century draws to a close, Tadoule Lake has no running water or sewage. A truck carries lake water across the community and fills the water tanks on every porch. There are "honey buckets" in bathrooms, buckets under kitchen sinks. People empty their buckets in the woods, in holes that they cover in spring with earth. They say their population is still too small to worry about contaminating the ground water and the lake.

Three satellite dishes standing on the hill behind Ila and Ernie Bussidor's house bring images from Bosnia, Palestine, and New York's Yankee Stadium into living rooms where meat racks still hang above woodstoves. Even Betsy Anderson has a colour television across from her bed/couch. She leaves it on in the afternoon — on mute since she can't understand English — while she does her beadwork. Images of women in designer suits and men in corporate boardrooms float and dissolve soundlessly on the screen in her cabin.

"When I look back now, I am amazed that our people survived the years in

Churchill when everything in our lives was destructive," Betsy Anderson says. "I am the oldest. People of my generation, and even generations after me, have all passed away. The Sayisi Dene I knew when I was young are gone. The people in our community today are 'new' people. I am the only one who knows the old and who is living with the 'new'." Indeed, in 1997, the Sayisi Dene of Tadoule Lake are a different people from the "Chipewyans," who, in faded archive photos, stand beside a tent and a row of pelts and whose dark eyes look at the camera out of chiselled, tawny faces.

Young people in Tadoule Lake pass winter evenings watching *Batman Forever* and *Pulp Fiction* on rented videos. Teenagers walk around with ear-phones, moving to the rhythm of Green Day and Sheryl Crow. They sport baggy clothes, Nike running shoes, Calvin Klein jeans. Sports jackets with professional team insignia such as the Chicago Bulls and the Los Angeles Raiders are in.

The twenty-first century is at the door, and technology has power over geographical isolation. The Sayisi Dene band office at Tadoule Lake is computerized. They have fax machines that depend on satellite connections. "We can take what we want, what we need, from technology," says Ernie Bussidor. "Sure we can use computers. A fast snowmobile will get you from point A to point B faster than snowshoes. These tools are important. As long as we revive our sense of independence, as long as we retain a sense of identity, technology will help us — not undermine our strength."

Like all First Nations bands in Manitoba, the Sayisi Dene band at Tadoule Lake is preparing for self-government. The Department of Indian Affairs, which had run people's lives for close to a century, is being dismantled. Bands are taking control of their own education, health services, social programs, and financial management, at a dizzying speed. Ernie said the process was exhilarating and scary at the same time:

> In a community the size of Tadoule Lake, dismantling Indian Affairs means local people have to get involved in administering all the services that were run by Indian Affairs until now. It's difficult because we are so few. Our bank of people to draw from is limited. You need people who have political knowledge, some economic knowledge, and who have an interest in administration. It's a colossal task. In our community, it's as if you're digging into a bag and pulling out the same people again and again. It puts tremendous pressure on the few people who have some education. They end up wearing two, three hats.

The times call for political, economic, and spiritual battles. Self-government can seem overwhelming for a community facing unemployment, a shortage of housing, drug abuse, family violence, and cultural degeneration — issues faced by most Aboriginal communities. To tackle them, people first have to begin to heal from past injuries. Ernie says, "Healing is a magic word for Tadoule Lake. You hear that word over and over in the North. We all long for healing. Not a sudden cure for our disease, but a gradual, repeated process of facing the past, expressing our pain and our anger and finding a flicker of new hope." At the word *hope*, Ernie pauses. "It's the hardest thing," he says. "Despair is so much easier."

> Long, long ago, there was a time of warfare between the Cree, the Inuit, and the Dene — a time of chaos. After that came a period when the caribou was abundant and the people lived in harmony. Now, we're going through an era when life is chaotic again. We've lost control of our land and our language. Our young people don't know their own history. I wonder how the new people will survive. When the elders think like this, the heart is sad. (Ronnie John Bussidor)

The drug trade has become a force of chaos in Tadoule Lake. The new airstrip has allowed increased traffic of drugs and bootlegged alcohol. Dealers are selling marijuana, cocaine, and acid. Many teenagers who can't afford those drugs are trying pills or sniffing. One weekend in the spring of 1996, a teenage girl armed with a knife broke into a teacher's house and attacked him. That afternoon, two teachers left the community. Ila says that Tadoule Lake is known as the dope centre of northern Manitoba. "The settlement's economy is based on dope pushing. The people who provide the dope don't see the fact that they're destroying another generation of people. The majority of people in Tadoule Lake live on welfare, and they spend a big part of it on dope. Many people here don't own anything — not even an ax or a saw. But they're addicted to dope and they exist just with a little bit of food and with dope. So many young people can't even go into the bush to get a load of wood because they're burnt out from drugs."

Drug dealers are gaining political power, interfering with band affairs. "There's so much tension in the community, it's hard to do anything constructive," Ernie says. "Caribou run just outside our windows. The geese are flying. The land is so beautiful. It's sad that the people don't see the beauty of the place. They've forgotten their respect for nature. Only a handful of elders are still alive, and they're so injured that they can't guide the young."

Ernie is discouraged by the problems that surface, by the pain that lingers and festers as years go by. He says demons, night spirits, seem to haunt the Sayisi Dene. "To heal together is a very difficult process, but we know it's necessary for our community because, if we don't heal, our injuries will pass on to our kids and our kids will pass them on to their children. People in Tadoule Lake live with such pain, such chronic anxiety, that it becomes unbearable. We have to nurture our sense of identity and strength. That's something you do again and again. Everyone has to struggle for it in their own way, at their own pace. Only if we can overcome the disruption of our lives caused by this baggage we carry from

Churchill will we be able to move forward. Our highest priority has to be soothing the souls of our people."

But how? When Ila was Drug and Alcohol Program worker at Tadoule Lake, she was discouraged when only four people showed up for a healing workshop she organized. Later, band members did participate in greater numbers in a healing circle, but Ila came to realize that large circles do not work — people hesitate to open up. She decided that the only way to build trust and support may be to start with a small group of two other women who already are close friends.

A few elders still praise the healing power of traditional spiritual practices, of the ancient drum songs and drum dances:

A long time ago, our people had spiritual power. Medicine people would go into a "shaking tent" when they were seeking visions and healing powers. They would sing this chant. The drum songs and sacred chants were beautiful sounds that aren't heard today. (Fred Duck)

Drums are good, they keep bad spirits away. The drum is not just an instrument, it helps the blood flow freely. In the past, the drum was used by knowledgeable people, medicine men, who used it with their songs to help people. Our people were among the most powerful. The Dene walked on water and wandered in the sky. The drum and their special songs gave them strength. (John Solomon)

A long time ago, the Sayisi Dene were very powerful with the medicine they had. It vanished from our people because it was too powerful. This medicine will return to our people again. My father said that two or three of our people will be given back this power. This was told to him by his elders many years ago. He said that the sacred tent, called the shaking tent — the poles from this have to be found and erected, and when this happens our medicine powers will return to us once again. (Eva Anderson)

The drum songs and drum dances — once a natural part of life — are now practised deliberately. All special events start with drum songs. A drum group meets regularly and participates in pow-wows and contests across the province. The drummers encourage teenage boys to learn the songs by organizing drum song contests for teens at the annual spring festival.

Some people still remember the ancient Dene hand game in which two teams of men sit on the ground facing each other and someone hides a pebble in his hand and passes the pebble from hand to hand with swift, stylized movements. The other team has to find the pebble. It's a fast-moving game of skill and concentration. Ernie Bussidor plays it and teaches it to others in Tadoule Lake.

In September 1995, the Sayisi Dene Education Committee began to control education funds, develop curriculum, choose educational goals, and hire teachers. For the first time in their history, the Sayisi Dene are teaching their own language and culture in school: "the things we took for granted and lost — things like our drum songs and dances, our traditional hand game. . . . A weak thread still holds those things in our memory. We want to strengthen that thread," says Ernie Bussidor.

Ernie's brother Jeff is the Dene language instructor. He has a tough job. Children want to learn their ancestral language, but they find it hard because their parents don't speak Dene at home. They can't. Jeff once sent out report cards in Dene syllabics to remind parents how much they had lost. "To this day, we don't know what that report card said," Ila says. "We're planning to set up Dene language courses for adults too. That's the only way we'll recover our language."

A generation of Sayisi Dene born after Churchill, like Ila's son Jason and her niece Sheila Thorassie, are now becoming adults. They are the "new people," who will carry their community into the future. They will not live off the land; they will need new political, administrative and economic skills to make their way in the world. But they will also need to know and to be proud of who they are.

The Sayisi Dene Education Committee has scheduled regular outings on the land guided by an elder who shows students how to make snowshoes, how to find directions in the wilderness, how to set fish nets, how to make a fire, how to butcher an animal — all the activities that had been a matter of survival for the Sayisi Dene only forty years ago. Beyond the twentieth century, those activities are unlikely to be necessary for survival, but they will always be reminders of past strength.

Betsy Anderson says, "I'm still around to tell you these stories. I must have been a very strong woman." Granny Betsy has known five generations of her people at a time of devastating change. As she nears the end of her journey, she and other elders see hope in offering their words to a generation of Dene children who may otherwise never know that their people "were once as strong and as free as the wild animals on this land."

Some mornings, Ila looks out her kitchen window and sees caribou trotting across the frozen lake and stopping in the snow to inspect the land and the sky, carrying their antlers like ancient crowns. The caribou no longer feed, warm, or shelter Ila's family. She looks at the graceful animals with wonder and with longing, straining to remember, as if the caribou might communicate some secret knowledge to make her and her people whole again. Unafraid, the animals stand in the open expanse of snow for several minutes before running towards the shelter of the spruce on the far shore.

On winter nights when the moon is full, a white light filters through a haze over the frozen lake. Lights move in the sky behind shifting clouds. When you breathe, you inhale tiny bits of ice. Snowmobiles lie behind the houses like sleeping animals, and an immense silence falls over the settlement.

This harsh and beautiful land is our home. We, the Sayisi Dene, have survived the twentieth century. We'll be here to greet the twenty-first. (Ila Bussidor)

APPENDIX

Deaths of Sayisi Dene, 1956-1977

From November 1956 to November 1977, a total of 117 members of the Sayisi Dene First Nation died. Of this number, thirty-two were children under the age of two, many of whom died from diseases such as pneumonia or meningitis. Nearly half of the Sayisi Dene of all ages who died during this period — fifty-four in all — died violently, from alcohol-related causes or as a result of living conditions at Camp-10 or Dene Village. These people are listed below. This list was compiled by Ila Bussidor and Eva Thorassie.

Date	Initials	Sex	Age	Cause
11/60	W.Y.	M	infant	house fire
11/60	N.Y.	M	3	house fire
11/60	C.Y.	M	1	house fire
09/61	S.T.	M	61	murder
10/62	S.C.	M	29	murder
07/63	J.A.	M	27	drowning
07/63	J.A.	M	22	drowning
12/63	D.A	F	infant	accident/alcohol-related
04/65	J.E.	F	26	died in jail
04/65	E.Y.	F	28	murder
06/65	B.E.	F	4	hit by car
07/65	D.Y.	M	53	accident/alcohol-related

Date	Initials	Sex	Age	Cause
08/66	S.E.	F	38	accident/alcohol-related
02/67	T.D.	M	1	malnutrition
02/67	M.D.	F	infant	malnutrition
04/67	J.J.	M	17	exposure
07/67	A.C.	M	20	accident
08/67	P.B.	M	32	exposure
02/68	G.O.	M	56	exposure
10/68	R.T.	M	48	hit by car
12/68	M.Y.	F	39	exposure
03/69	P.M.	M	17	exposure
07/69	M.K.	M	69	neglect
09/69	M.M.	F	43	murder
04/70	A.C.	F	10	rheumatic fever
10/70	P.P.	M	55	exposure
12/70	M.D.	F	19	murder
05/71	I.O.	F	43	murder
01/71	M.Y.	M	5	house fire
01/71	R.Y.	M	3	house fire
01/71	D.Y.	F	2	house fire
07/71	E.B.	M	12	presumed murdered
08/71	A.Y.	F	81	hit by car
11/71	E.M.	F	37	alcohol-related
12/71	C.T.	M	49	exposure
05/72	J.M.	M	31	alcohol-related
09/72	P.E.	M	37	hit by car
12/72	A.C.	M	66	house fire
12/72	S.C.	F	50	house fire
07/63	A.T.	F	69	house fire
09/73	G.Y.	M	54	alcohol-related
09/73	M.B.	F	44	food poisoning
01/74	A.Y.	F	14	missing since 1974
10/74	B.E.	M	17	murder
02/75	O.T.	M	17	murder
09/75	S.E.	F	39	alcohol-related
10/75	J.T.	M	41	hit by car
07/76	D.B.	M	28	drowning
07/76	L.T.	M	7	drowning
07/76	J.J.	M	17	drowning
11/77	R.C.	M	18	house fire
11/77	R.J.	F	24	house fire
11/77	J.J.	M	4	house fire
11/77	J.J.	M	2	house fire

NOTES

The People from the East
1. Petch, "Relocation," 6.
2. Abel, *Drum Songs*, xiv-xvi.
3. Their seasonal round was in synchrony with the Beverly Kaminuriak herd (Petch, "Relocation," 1).
4. Abel, *Drum Songs*, 24, 25.
5. Ibid., 45.
6. Ibid., 46.
7. Ibid., 43-64.
8. Ibid., 63.
9. Hearne, *Journey*, 115.
10. Ibid., 50-52.
11. Petch, "Relocation," 9-10.
12. Abel, *Drum Songs*, 113-144.
13. Betsy Anderson and other Dene-speaking elders use the word *bonlai* to refer to Euro-Canadians. *Bonlai* has been translated as "white men" or "white people".

Treaty Five
1. This discussion of the adhesions to Treaty Five and its background is based largely on chapter 5 of Tough, *"As Their Natural Resources Fail"*, 99-113.
2. Treaty text quoted in ibid, 318.
3. Ibid., 99.
4. Ibid., 109.
5. Ibid.

Duck Lake

1. Acting Indian Agent J.H. Hellofs (January 9, 1928), quoted in Tough, *"As Their Natural Resources Fail,"* 292.
2. Godsell, *Arctic Trader,* 196-197.
3. Abel, *Drum Songs,* 188.
4. Ibid., 190.
5. Elias, *Metropolis and Hinterland,* 13.
6. Abel, *Drum Songs,* 210.
7. Ibid., 199.
8. NAC, RG 10, v. 4093, f. 600, 138, Reverend A.D. Dewdney to Scott, November 14, 1925.
9. Petch, "Relocation," 20.
10. Lal, "From Duck Lake to Camp 10," 9.

"Preserved at all Costs"

1. See: Abel, *Drum Songs,* 214-230.
2. Petch, "Relocation," 22-23.
3. Virginia Petch, interview.
4. Banfield, "The Caribou Crisis," 4-6.
5. NAC, RG 109, v. 402, f. WLU 222-228[2], "Resumé of the First Caribou Conservation Meeting," Saskatoon, October 13, 1955, 5.
6. Banfield, "The Caribou Crisis," 7.
7. G.H. Gooderham, Regional Supervisor of Indian Agencies in the Northwest Territories, September 14, 1949, quoted in Abel, *Drum Songs,* 223.

The Relocation

1. Miller, *Skyscrapers Hide the Heavens,* 221-222.
2. HBCA RG 3173A14.
3. DIAND 138/329-2, R.H. Chesshire of the HBC to Colonel Jones, Director, Department of Citizenship and Immigration at the Indian Affairs Branch in Ottawa, June 28, 1956.
4. DIAND 138/29-2, July 12, 1956.
5. Ibid.
6. Ibid.
7. Ibid.
8. Ibid.
9. Minutes, The Pas, Manitoba, September 10, 1956, 8.
10. Mary Ila Code, "A Brief History and Geography," 21.
11. DIAND 138/29-2.

Churchill

1. Allan Code and Mary Code, "Deaths and Causes," 2.
2. Elias, *Metropolis and Hinterland,* 17.
3. DIAND 138/29-2, Malcolmson letter, May 24, 1957.
4. DIAND 138/20-4, W.R. Burns to Mr. M. Kartushyn, Assistant Indian Agency in Churchill.
5. DIAND 138/29-2-2, J.R. Tully to R.D. Ragan.
6. Ibid.
7. Ibid.
8. PAM, memorandum from R.W. Gyles, Director of Lands, July 15, 1957.
9. DIAND 138/29-2 [r.7], W.C. Bethune to R.D. Ragan, July 31, 1957.

Camp-10

1. According to DIAND correspondence, a small house would have cost approximately $10,000. The cabins at Camp-10 cost $765 each.

2. Koolage, "Chipewyan Indians of Camp-10," 83-84.
3. Virginia Petch, interview.

Alcohol Takes Over

1. Petch, "Relocation," 40-41.
2. Diocese of Keewatin Archive, letter from Bishop Hives to Director of Nursing, Fisher Branch Hospital, 1962.
3. NAC, RG 10, v. 4093, f. 600, 135/29-2-2, Chief John Clipping to Archie Leslie, Regional Director of Indian Affairs, July 26, 1963, 2.
4. Koolage, "Chipewyan Indians of Camp-10," 74.
5. Ibid., 75.

Dene Village

1. According to *Community Development Study for the Churchill Band of Indians: Dene Village* (Winnipeg: Underwood, McLellan and Associates Ltd., 1967, 22), nineteen children were away in foster homes.
2. DIAND OTT 578/30-54, v. 1, Minutes of Band Council Meeting, Churchill Band, September 15, 1966.
3. DIAND 501/29-2, R.F. Battle to the Minister, September 21, 1966.
4. Dickman, "Thoughts on Relocation," 25.
5. Phil Dickman, interview.
6. Dickman, "Thoughts on Relocation," 21.
7. Ibid., 25.
8. Virginia Petch, interview.
9. *Taiga Times*, January 30, 1967.

Deaths

1. Special Consultation, Royal Commission on Aboriginal Peoples (RCAP), 4.
2. *Taiga Times*, February 1, 1971.

Return to the Land

1. Dickman, "Thoughts on Relocation," 25.
2. Phil Dickman, interview.
3. Dickman, "Thoughts on Relocation," 23.
4. Ibid., 28.
5. Phil Dickman, interview.
6. Ibid.
7. Dickman, "Thoughts on Relocation," 30.
8. Phil Dickman, interview.
9. DIAND 578/3-6-303, v. 1, A. Sandberry to R.M. Connelly.
10. Bob Lowery, "Manitoba's Newest Community Getting Ready for Christmas," *Winnipeg Free Press*, December 1973.

Tadoule Lake

1. Ila Bussidor, presentation to RCAP.
2. RCAP, "Looking Forward, Looking Back," 430-431.
3. Ibid., 438.

BIBLIOGRAPHY

Books, Articles, Dissertations

Abel, Kerry. *Drum Songs: Glimpses of Dene History*. Montreal: McGill-Queen's University Press, 1993.

Banfield, A.W.F. "The Caribou Crisis," *The Beaver* (spring 1956):3-7.

Birket-Smith, Kaj. *Contributions to Chipewyan Ethnology: Report of the Fifth Thule Expedition, 1921-24*. Copenhagen: Gyldendalske Boghandel, Nordisk Forlag, 1930.

Brandson, Lorraine E. *From Tundra to Forest: A Chipewyan Resource Manual*. Winnipeg: Manitoba Museum of Man and Nature, 1981.

Bruemmer, F. "Life After Degradation." *Weekend Magazine*, January 8, 1977.

Dickman, Phil. "Thoughts on Relocation." *The Musk-Ox* 6 (1971):21-31.

_____. "North Knife Lake." *The Musk-Ox* 8 (1971):27-30.

Elias, Peter Douglas. *Metropolis and Hinterland in Northern Manitoba*. Winnipeg: Manitoba Museum of Man and Nature, 1975.

Godsell, Philip. *Arctic Trader: The Account of Twenty Years with the Hudson's Bay Company*. New York: G.P. Putnam and Sons, 1934.

Harrington, Lyn. *Manitoba Roundabout*. Toronto: Ryerson Press, 1951.

Hearne, Samuel. *A Journey from Prince of Wales's Fort in Hudson Bay to the Northern Ocean in the Years 1769, 1779, 1771 and 1772*. Edited with an introduction by Richard Glover. Toronto: Macmillan Company of Canada, 1958.

Keighley, Sidney A. *Tripper, Trapper, Trader: The Life of a Bay Man*. Winnipeg: Watson and Dwyer Publishing, 1989.

Kenney, James F. *The Founding of Churchill*. London: J.M. Dent and Sons, 1932.

Kenyon, Walter. *The Journal of Jens Munk, 1619-1620*. Toronto: Royal Ontario Museum, 1980.

Koolage, William W., Jr. "Adaptation of Chipeywan Indians and Other Persons of Native Background in Churchill, Manitoba." PhD dissertation, University of North Carolina at Chapel Hill, 1970.

_____. "Chipewyan Indians of Camp-10." In *Ethnographic Survey of Churchill*, edited by John J. Honigman. Chapel Hill: Institute for Research in Social Science, University of North Carolina at Chapel Hill, 1968.

Lal, Ravindra. "From Duck Lake to Camp 10: Old Fashioned Relocation." *The Musk-Ox* 6 (1969):5-13.

_____. "Some Observations on the Social Life of the Chipewyans of Camp-10, Churchill, and their Implications for Community Development." *The Musk-Ox* 6 (1969):14-20.

Miller, J.R. *Skyscrapers Hide the Heavens: A History of Indian-White Relations in Canada.* Toronto: University of Toronto Press, 1991.

Tough, Frank. *"As Their Natural Resources Fail": Native Peoples and the Economic History of Northern Manitoba, 1870-1930.* Vancouver: University of British Columbia Press, 1996.

Archival Material

Archives of the Anglican Church, Diocese of Keewatin, Kenora, Ontario.
Archives of the Churchill Museum (Churchill, Manitoba).
Archives of the Churchill Public Library.
Department of Indian Affairs and Northern Development (DIAND).
Hudson's Bay Company Archives (HBCA).
National Archives of Canada (NAC).
Provincial Archives of Manitoba (PAM).

Newspapers

The Taiga Times, Churchill, Manitoba (between 1960 and 1972)
Winnipeg Free Press

Videotapes

Aboriginal Justice Inquiry. Videotapes of Hearings at Tadoule Lake, Manitoba. January 12, 1989, Provincial Archives of Manitoba.

Code, Allan. *Nu Ho Ni Yeh: Our Story.* Treeline Productions, Tadoule Lake, Manitoba, 1993.

Reports, Background Papers, Studies

Bussidor, Ila. Presentation to the Royal Commission on Aboriginal Peoples (RCAP), Thompson, Manitoba, June 1, 1993. Transcript.

Canada. Royal Commission on Aboriginal Peoples (RCAP). Report. Volume 1, "Looking Forward, Looking Back." Ottawa: Canada Communications Group, 1996.

Code, Allan, and Mary Code. "Deaths and Causes, Sayisi Dene First Nation, Fort Churchill Band, 1956-1993." Unpublished report, 1995.

Code, Mary Ila. "A Brief History and Geography of the Sayisi Dene and Their Land." Tadoule Lake. Unpublished paper.

Hlady, Walter. "A Community Development Project amongst the Churchill Band at Churchill, Manitoba, September 1959 to March 1960." Unpublished report. Saskatoon, 1960.

Petch, Virginia. "The Relocation of the Sayisi Dene of Tadoule Lake." Background paper prepared for the Royal Commission on Aboriginal Peoples, 1995.

Royal Commission on Aboriginal Peoples (RCAP), Report on Special Consultation, Tadoule Lake Manitoba, October 19, 1993.

Windborn Consulting (Douglas M. Skoog with Ian R. Macmillan). Band Relocation Study, 1991.